PILLARS OF THE PENTAGON

Nita Scoggan

*To my friend,
Connie
God bless you honey!
Love,
Nita Scoggan*

ROYALTY PUBLISHING COMPANY
P.O. Box 2016   Manassas, Virginia, 22110

Royalty Publishing Company
P.O. Box 2016
Manassas, Virginia 22110

Printed in the United States of America

FIRST EDITION

Library of Congress Catalog Number: 82-050507

ISBN 0-934588-05-8

All Scripture quotes are from King James Version (KJV) unless otherwise noted.

"Daughters of graceful beauty

like pillars of a palace wall"

Psalms 144:12
(Living Bible)

The Mall Entrance
Pentagon Building

Nita Scoggan '81

Pentagon Pillars

Nita Scoggan

Lagoon

Nita Scoggan

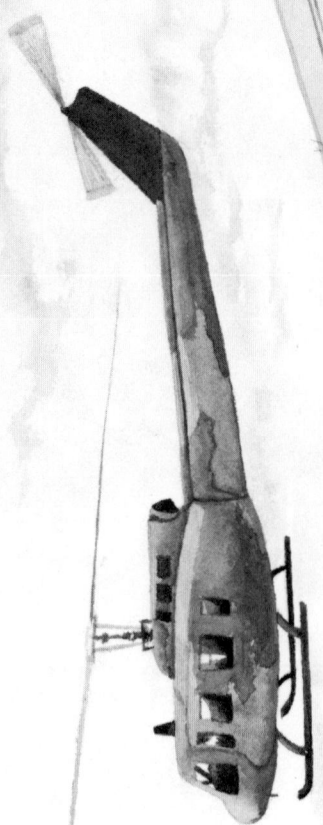

Heliport

Nita Scoggan

The Mall Entrance
Pentagon Building

Nita Scoggan '81

Mall Entrance

Nita Scoggan

South Parking Entrance

Nita Scoggan

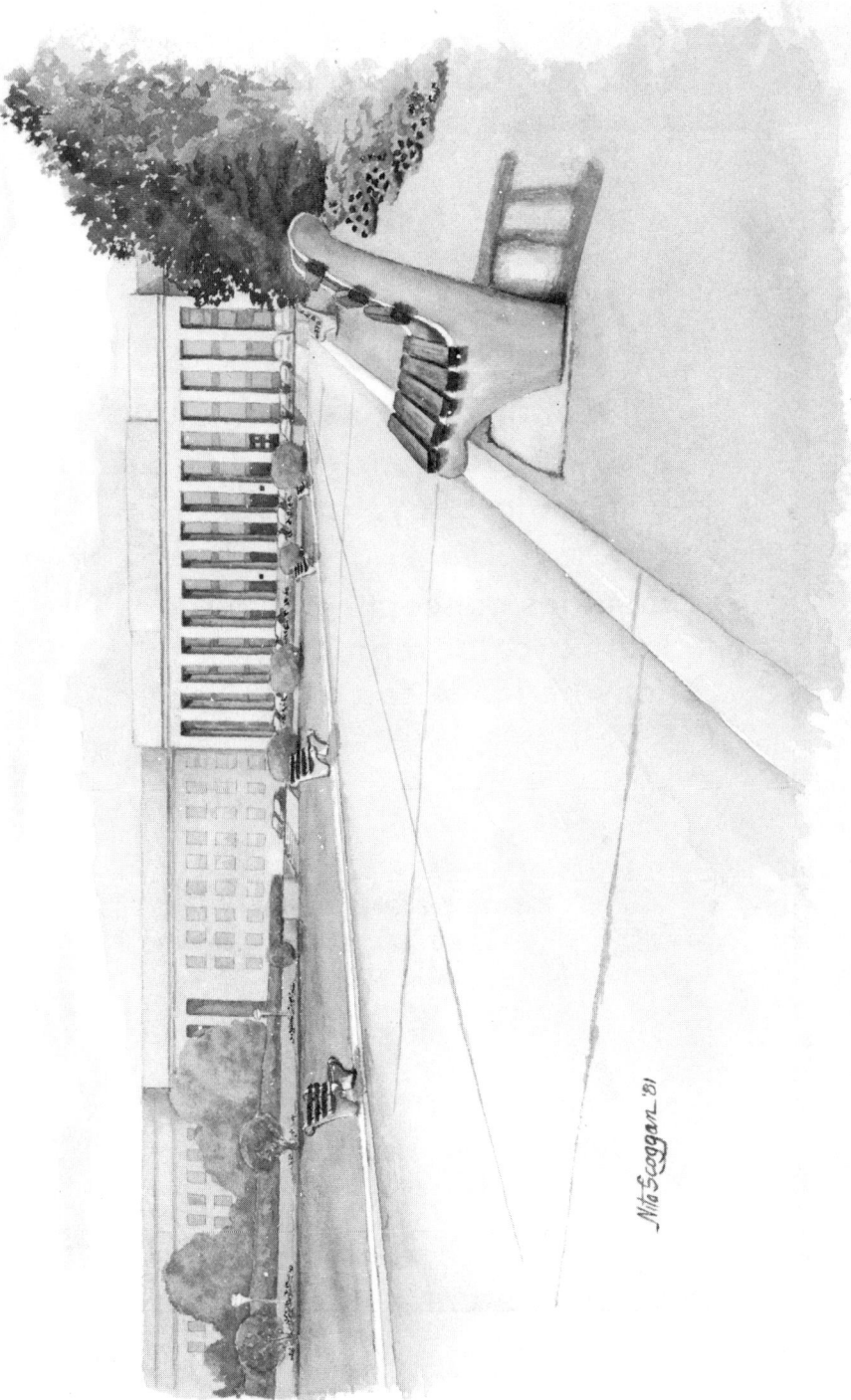

River Entrance

Nita Scoggan

All paintings in this publication
are reproductions from original
watercolors by Nita Scoggan

Inquiries concerning Limited
Edition color reproductions
may be made to the Publisher

ROYALTY PUBLISHING COMPANY
P.O. BOX 2016
Manassas, Va., 22110

Pillars of the Pentagon

TABLE OF CONTENTS

Page

Acknowledgements

With constant thanks to the Lord for making it possible to get this story out of my heart and into print, I affirm that I can do nothing without Him!

Grateful appreciation is given to:

* My best friend, my husband, Bill, who has loved me, listened, and encouraged me; without his constant support this book would never have been completed.
* My friend, Irene Burk Harrell, whose encouragement inspired me to put pen to paper and begin writing.
* My friends, Susie Ezzell, Jean Johnson, Amelia Richardson, Claudia Burrell, Jula Kesner and Cindy Mulroney, who cheerfully typed and retyped, after deciphering my writing!
* My friends, Cecil Webb for his beautiful photographs and Mr. Ben Chaney for the good suggestions he offered.
* My friends, Nettie Sides, John Broger, and Sgt. First Class Mike Mulroney, for their assistance in research.
* My dear friend, Maidie Stanley, whose faithfulness and love inspired this story.
* My dear sister, Hazel, whose love for Jesus and others has inspired my faith; and her love for me has been invaluable.
* My dear Mother, Delma Jenkins, whose love, hard work and generosity encouraged me through my lifetime.

These friends and family have been a real gift from the Lord!

Nita Scoggan

FOREWORD

NO TIME TO WRITE A BOOK!

"You really ought to write a book about the Pentagon," Major General Jerry Curry, United States Army, said to me, "about the women and the activities here."

"You've got to be kidding!" I replied. "I can't write a book, I don't know how."

"It isn't necessary! There are good people who will help you." General Curry continued, "I have a friend, Irene Harrell, who would be perfect! I'll give you her address, if you are interested."

General Curry was smiling and so enthusiastic, I knew he expected me to ask for it, right then and there! My husband, Bill, and I were standing behind the General in a reception line, in the Pentagon. I looked at Bill, who was smiling too. This was serious business! Me...writing a book?

"You know, General Curry," I told him, "you are the seventh person who has told me that I should write a book about the Pentagon Ladies."

"You really ought to pray about it," he replied. "I will. I really will," I concluded.

The conversation changed to retirement, and General Curry wanted to know how Bill was enjoying his recent decision, and what he was finding to do to keep active. The subject turned to gardening and lawn care.

If anyone ever contemplated retirement and had any hesitation, they needed to talk with my husband! He thoroughly enjoyed every minute and stayed so busy doing little projects and hobbies, he didn't have time to get bored. He loved the outdoors and had put in a lovely Azalea bed, which he described to General Curry.

"Let me tell you, Bill," the General said, "I know all about gardening! My wife, Charlene, wanted a flower bed put in, she kept talking about it and how nice it would look."

He continued, "Finally, I decided to take a Saturday and make her happy, by doing that for her."

"You know, Charlene is writing a book, don't you?" He asked. We did, and asked how "The General's Lady" was coming along. "Fine," was his brief comment; he was anxious to tell his gardening story.

"Bill, I worked for hours in the hot sun. I had to use a pickaxe! That ground was like cement." He was warming up to his story -- smiling from ear to ear.

"I worked for six hours. I didn't even take a break. I knew she'd be so happy. I knew she'd be proud of my efforts," he told us. "Do you know what happened?"

"I finally called her out, to look at the finished flower beds, and she came to the door. She didn't even come outside! She had her notebook and pen in her hand, and she came to the door. She was busy writing her book -- she didn't have time to come out and look at the flowers," his story went on. "She just looked out at the yard and pointed."

"I told you I wanted this over here," she told him, "and those over there."

"Bill, with that, she turned and went back to writing her book!" General Curry laughed, "She acted just like a General!"

That little incident, told in an amusing manner by our friend, caused me to wonder how I could ever find time to write a book!

I am employed full time, with a husband and home to keep me busy. After those hours of responsibilities are finished, I have no time to write a book!

My lunch hours are taken up with the various Bible studies and prayer groups I've written about. I feel I'm not to neglect these, but continue to be faithful to attend. So...No time to write a book!

On weekends my husband likes to do things with me, and I love it! So, no time to write a book!

Sunday is "for the Lord" and after Church we rest; we've found long ago we need it. So, no time to write a book!

But God has given me time to write a book. It has to be God's doing. I've written every morning, and every evening, as I travel to the Pentagon and home again.

Could anyone write a book, juggling a notepad on your knee, as you jostle along in traffic? The vanpool members were skeptical, but encouraging. With winter months and early gloom, I began bringing a flashlight, so I could see to write!! They were really supportive. Col. Ron Lane suggested I use the reading light over my seat...it was lots easier than the flashlight...but kept some of them from napping.

Only God could make people so cooperative!

Only God could give me two hours a day, free from phones, and responsibilities...so I could write a book! I'm giving God the credit for doing it. "Faithful is He who has called you (to write a book), who also will do it." (1 Thess. 5:24)

Nita Scoggan

Chapter 1

WEIGHING IN AT TWO POUNDS

"Don't bother to give her a name...she won't live." The Doctor spoke these somber words, after a difficult delivery, to the young woman lying in bed.

It was a hot August night, typical of west Texas in the summer. The year was 1927, in a small town of Cisco. The Doctor packed his black bag, he was ready to leave the house to which he had been called that night, and return to his own home and bed. He finished wiping his hands and turned to the Grandmother, who was standing nearby.

"Two pounds is just too small, so we won't take the baby to the Hospital to put her in the Incubator. She is just too premature to live...I'm sorry," he said.

"Is there anything we should do for the baby?" the Grandmother asked. She was so distressed over the situation and worried about her daughter and the baby, which wasn't given any chance to live. This wasn't a pretty baby. She had no fingernails, toenails nor any hair. Just red and wrinkled and too weak to cry.

"Try to keep her warm," the Doctor replied, "and get a little milk into her if you can. I think she is too weak to nurse, but you can try."

As he neared the front door to leave the Doctor said, "Give me a call in the morning and we will take care of the papers. Let me know how your daughter is doing. Goodnight."

The young woman, Delma, had been hitch-hiking all that day to reach her Mother's home. She had run off and gotten married and then her husband had deserted her when it neared the time for her to have a baby. She had no money, but wanted to get home, so she stood by the roadside for hours, hoping someone would give her a ride. The sun was hot and she felt so uncomfortable, every minute seemed like an hour. Finally someone stopped; but they were only going part of the way. Still she was grateful to get that much closer to home. The day wore on, more standing, more walking in the blazing heat. Delma felt sick when she arrived, unannounced and unexpected, at her

1

Mother's house. Later that night the labor pains began and the Doctor had come to the house.

A week passed by. The Grandmother fed the new infant with an eyedropper, and kept her in diapers made from some of her dainty handkerchiefs. She had fixed up a shoe box with cotton and kept the baby warm. She was still alive...it was a miracle!

"We have decided to give the baby a name," the Grandmother told the Doctor over the phone, "she is still alive!" The Doctor was amazed and asked to have the new Mother and the baby brought in for a check-up, and to fill out a Birth certificate. "Juanita Lee is the name," Delma said, and the Doctor completed the papers, "I want to name her Lee, after my Father and I've always liked the name Juanita."

"God must want this baby to live," the Grandmother said. The Doctor nodded and replied, "Evidently God did. She didn't have a chance to live, but He gave her a chance."

And so life began for a tiny, weak baby girl, who weighed two pounds at birth. It was a life of sleepless nights for Delma, as she would be up caring for a sickly child. Me!

There were constant breathing difficulties, colds and Pneumonia at two years of age, which almost ended the story before my life got off to a good start!

Delma was reconcilled and Hazel was born, happy and healthy 8 pounds at birth. The Doctors diagnosed my problems as asthma, allergies, hay fever, sinus and other difficulties which kept me underweight, pale, coughing, sneezing, wheezing and sleepless. The nights were the worst. No amount of cough syrup, medication, spanking nor coaxing helped. I just coughed and struggled for breath, even propped to an almost sitting position. Tonsils and adenoids were removed without any improvement and there was talk of extensive surgery in the sinus canals, so I could breathe through my nose instead of gasping for air between bites as I tried to eat.

Then disaster struck!

* * * *

Heavy rains caused the rivers to rise above flood stage, and still the rain continued to fall...by dawn the town was almost cut off from the surrounding area. The rain came without warning, homes and roads were under water.

Even though I was seven years old, I recall what it was like.

I woke up hearing rain on the roof and got out of bed and stepped into water! There was water everywhere! No one was awake; but I ran into my parents room telling them excitedly about water all over the house. There was no time to lose. My step-father had us put on a dress and we ran out of our house toward the City Hall building, which was the highest point in our town of San Angelo, Texas.

Little did we know that we would never be able to go back to our home again. We didn't even have any shoes on! We had literally run for our lives. So had most of the other residents of the town. The

City Hall building was crowded, and it was to remain that way for several days, till the flood waters receded.

Thinking about it now, it seems like a bad dream. People were crying all around me. I can remember looking out the windows at houses floating down the river and smashing into the bridge and disappearing from sight. I can still hear people screaming hysterically over those awesome scenes. The streets were like little rivers. I remember seeing all kinds of things floating past the windows -- trunks, furniture, cars.

I thought of the trunks in our house and wondered if they were still there. My parents could only hope so. One trunk had our dolls and toys...I surely wanted to get home and play with them again. Another trunk had my new school dresses and the beautiful Shirley Temple coats and hats that Mother had just gotten out of layaway. I was going to be in second grade and was looking forward to school, especially anticipating the pretty dresses Mother had made for me to wear. I wanted to look like Shirley Temple. My sister Hazel did, with her naturally curly hair and dimples. I was skin and bones and had straight hair, but I could dream! And when I put on a beautiful dress with lots of ruffles I was just sure I looked like Shirley, too.

Another trunk had our family pictures, photo albums and keepsakes. They were gone. Everything was gone. I can remember the Salvation Army providing some hot food. The school building had floors that were "wavy" and a high brown line up near the ceiling where the water had been! But the building was still there and we did get to go to school. Only now I didn't have any clothes except what was given to me. I cried over the loss of my pretty dresses and dolls. My Mother cried a lot, too. We lost everything.

Before long we were on our way to start a new life in California. I recall riding in my Uncle Calvin's car. It was beautiful and he was very proud of his Buick. We didn't own a car and I was sure my uncle was rich. I was glad we were going to California. Maybe we would be rich too! Other people went to California and got into the movies. Maybe I would be in the movies. I liked to dance and dreamed I would be like Ginger Rogers or Eleanor Powell and tap my way to stardom. The fact that I was still skin and bones, 8 years old and sick a lot didn't influence my daydreams one bit. Neither did my straight hair...I still dreamed I'd have Shirley Temple curls.

Life in California was different for us. For the next few years, Mother had to work every day and we lived in an apartment instead of a house. But Hazel and I were good playmates. We enjoyed Los Angeles and going where movie stars appeared in glamorous clothes and bright lights, hoping to get their autographs. Going to the famous Rose Parade and just being near Hollywood was pretty exciting stuff to talk about in school.

Meanwhile things weren't going so well in school for me. We moved a good bit and I was never able to understand all the school work. I can remember Mom and Dad trying to help me in the evenings, and Hazel would catch on before I did. I looked forward to recess and loved to play softball and dodge-ball, or anything that had to do

3

with climbing or jumping. I was so limber people said I was double-jointed, I wasn't sure just what that meant, but I liked being able to do flips and cartwheels. But for some reason, my asthma became worse than ever. I coughed up great gobs of phlegm and was back to wheezing and painful breathing, sneezing and the whole works.

The school consulted my parents and medical check-ups were required. Before long I was no longer permitted to join others in recess! I had to go and lay down in the Teachers Lounge while everyone else played outdoors. It didn't seem to help much. The coughing was so embarassing, and the gobs of phlegm gagged me, not to mention the pain in my chest. I was in the 6th grade now and humiliated at being sick and unable to join my classmates at recess activities.

My "rich" Uncle Calvin came to see us and took us for drives on Sunday afternoons and bought us ice cream cones. It was the highlight of our week when he would come to visit. Occasionally we would go to his house for dinner. He had a beautiful wife, daughter and home. I was sure he had everything! Besides he was jolly and fun to be with. I thought that someday I would be a movie star and have a beautiful home and a car just like Uncle Calvin's. I wanted to live in Hollywood forever.

You can imagine my dismay when my Dad and Mother began talking about moving to Alaska! All I had ever heard about Alaska was the igloo homes and Eskimos with their dog teams. I didn't want to go! I protested and cried to no avail. My Dad accepted the job of Special Agent with the Alaska Railroad and left Los Angeles to explore this "new frontier" before he sent for Mother, Hazel and myself to join him. The year was 1938.

Dad's letters from Alaska were full of excitement and love for this great country and fine people that he had met. He admired their ingenuity and skill in clearing land and building their own homes, eating wild game they had hunted and fish they had caught from the streams. He was hooked on Alaska and said he would never leave. He wanted to build a home and settle down.

In 1939 my Mother sold or packed up everything and sent Hazel and I to Texas to stay with grandmother for a year, while she joined Dad. After they had built us a house, she would come and get us. Mother sounded just as enthusiastic as Dad about going to a new land where there were few people and you could just be yourself. They were tired of Hollywood, cocktail parties and all that went with it.

The year passed quickly into two and we were shocked to learn that the Japanese had attacked Pearl Harbor and we were at war! I was in high school and heard the older boys talking of having to go and fight. Somehow it all seemed so distant, I couldn't quite grasp what was really happening.

But Mother's letters shocked me into reality. The civilians were being shipped out of Alaska. They expected the Japanese to invade. Only those in essential work could remain. I didn't want my parents to stay up there and be killed! But Dad felt it was his duty to stay there and keep that small stretch of railroad functioning to supply the interior with necessary goods. He was considered "essential." He wanted Hazel and I there with them, so they made all the

4

arrangements and soon we had our train tickets. Dad would meet us in Seattle.

It's a far piece from Texas to Seattle, for two young girls, 14 and 12 years of age, who had never travelled alone anywhere. The trains were full of young men in military uniforms who had priority over other passengers, but God looked after us and protected us from all harm and danger during those days and nights of travel. We were too naive to realize that we may have been in danger. When we arrived in Seattle, Dad let us know quickly that our days of "freedom" were over! Those young G.I.s were going to war and they were looking for all the fun they could find, and he kept us under his watchful eye every minute.

We had a few days wait till the boat left for Alaska, as there would have to be a security convoy to accompany the ship. Many ships had been sunk by submarines and there was real danger. Dad told us of the blackouts in Alaska, where you had to have heavy black curtains over windows and not even strike a match outdoors, for it could be spotted by planes or troops. We began to understand that war was touching our lives and it was serious.

Our voyage to Anchorage was in October 1942. The ship was completely full of troops, except for a school teacher, my Dad, my sister and I, and the crew. We had daily lifeboat drills, and warnings to watch for submarines, plus the blackout procedures at night. No lights were allowed except in areas where the windows were covered. It was frightening. And my Dad didn't let us girls out of the stateroom except for meals. He wasn't going to tempt any of those young soldiers to flirt or be friendly with us.

Gale force winds and huge swells caused most of the meals to be omitted one day at sea. We thought of it as a roller coaster ride...somehow we didn't realize the danger. Hazel and I laughed because others were sick and we weren't.

Arriving in Seward, we boarded the Alaska Railroad that we had heard so much about and headed for Anchorage. Dad made the trip exciting by telling us that we would be seeing Polar Bears at every turn and we'd learn to love our igloo and dog sled. The only truth to the stories he told us, we learned, was about having to chop wood for the stove and carry water. We had the happy surprise to see modern buildings in Anchorage and that we had a real house to live in! Not an igloo! How proud we were of it...it was beautiful...and Mom and Dad had built it themselves. It was made of logs that had been peeled and oiled, so that the wood glistened. We loved it.

It was so wonderful to be with Mother again. She was more beautiful than we had remembered. We were so happy to be together, we forgot about the war...until the first weekend.

Dad told us that we were going to learn to shoot a gun. We were a long way from town and there were many reports of rape and murder involving the young soldiers who were stationed nearby. Dad wasn't taking any chances. He taught us to shoot and gave us orders to do so, if anyone tried to break in when we were home alone, while he and Mother were at work. Praise God, we never had to use any of these skills.

5

Wartime in Alaska made high school activities very limited. Martial law was imposed which meant a curfew. Civilians weren't to be on the streets after 7 p.m. without a valid reason, and youth were to be accompanied by an adult. With the curfew restrictions and the few hours of daylight in the winter months, we didn't have many school functions, but we did get outdoors to attend school, chop wood, carry water...or use the little house out back! Always in our minds was the fear of bombing attacks or invasion by the Japanese. We listened to the shortwave radio every evening to keep up with the daily events taking place in far off places. One of the far off places I heard mentioned was the Pentagon. Alaska was just a territory then and Washington D.C. seemed a world away.

Years passed and the war was over! I was nearing graduation from high school and planning to marry my high school sweetheart. I loved Alaska and shared my parents desire to make Alaska my home forever.

Where else could we go fishing and have huge Salmon jump out of the river and onto the banks for us to snag? Where else could we see wild game walking near our house? Where else could we see bits of the glittering stuff dreams were made of, when we'd go "panning for gold" in the mountain streams? Where else could we enjoy Dog Sled rides, ice fishing or hunting Moose, Caribou or Bear? Where else could my Dad work out in isolated villages, often the only white man the Eskimo had seen, and bring home all the exciting tales that went along with investigating crimes, as a Deputy Marshal? Though Anchorage was modern, a few miles away it was wilderness, without roads or communications. It was a frontier!

Upon graduation I accepted a job with the Federal Government, never dreaming that one day I would work in the biggest office building in the world...the Pentagon!

Chapter 2

FROM ALASKA TO THE PENTAGON

In March of 1953, I arrived in Union Station, with my two small sons, thus ending an unhappy teenage marriage that had begun in Anchorage, Alaska, seven years prior. I wanted to start a new life for myself, as far from Alaska as possible!

I had come with no money, to "visit" my only sister, Hazel, and her husband M/Sgt. Art Allaire. Art was stationed at Andrews Air Force Base outside Washington, D.C. They welcomed us to share their tiny apartment near the base until I could get a job.

I had worked for the Federal Government for two years, after high school, doing Architectural drafting. I got a job with the Government the first day I went looking! It was only "temporary" they told me, a GS-3 (on a scale of 1 to 18), in the Pentagon. I needed the job and I took it.

Little did I realize then that my "temporary job" would lead to a 30-year career with the Government, and almost every bit of it in the Pentagon!

I was overwhelmed by the Washington, DC traffic after the pioneer atmosphere I'd had for 10 years in Alaska! It took me more than two hours to get to work, using two buses. Besides a lot of walking and more of the same getting back home at night. Suburban living had its drawbacks!

What a confusing place the Pentagon was, I got lost every day for a week, just trying to find the restroom and cafeterias! But people were so friendly, they were quick to help a bewildered newcomer. Before long I was able to help others myself.

I started taking my boys, Lew and Steve, to Sunday School, at a tiny Methodist Church nearby. I took my two little nieces, Glenne and Lisa, too. Art was Catholic and Hazel had joined the Church when they got married in Anchorage. But they never went to church. All the children enjoyed Sunday School and before long I was asked to help teach a children's class due to the shortage of teachers. I certainly wasn't qualified, but willing. They gave me a Teacher's

Quarterly and I began teaching. I'm sure I learned more than the kids did!

Weekends, I would try to take the boys sightseeing downtown. Lew was five and Steve was two years old. Somehow I didn't really think I'd be in Washington long. So we took lots of pictures and went to see everything. We were sharing a big house with Hazel and Art then, and they were so good to us, but I knew they needed a "break."

Hazel watched my boys and her girls all week, while I worked. She was an ideal mother...I simply marvelled at her patience and just enjoying the kids. She'd make cookies and popsicles, and she'd play with them or let them make tents out of her blankets on rainy days. It didn't seem to bother her one bit if they "tore the house up." She would laugh and sing and straighten up later. Hazel and Art filled a desperate need in our life for stability and a home full of love.

At work, I was being trained by a young man, who was my supervisor. He was very hard to work for! He was very demanding and everything had to be extremely accurate. But I found he was very likeable. One other woman coworker, Kate Bratton, called him "Scoggan". Most of the men called him "Willy" -- they liked him, too. He'd come from a farm in Indiana, with lots of family back there. He was going through a divorce too. We had a lot of things to talk about and we enjoyed each other's companionship.

The first few times he asked me out I said "no," because I didn't want to be away from my boys any more than I already was, just working. But when he wanted to take us all on a picnic, to the beach...I changed my mind. He was not only nice to be with...he liked my children, too.

I discovered he had "Willy" written on his arm, and he said they'd called him that as he grew up. His first name was Paul. I really liked that name, but he didn't, so I called him Bill.

I really liked Bill, but we both agreed that we didn't ever want to get married again! Let's just stay friends!

Things changed in 1955, when Art was transferred to Japan, and Hazel and Glenne and Lisa left, too. Our little apartment was pretty lonely, and it was a terrible loss for my sons, Lew and Steve.

"Uncle Art" had been a real father figure to them. He was jolly and teased them all the time. They really missed him, and no one could replace "Aunt Hazel," especially me, when I'd come home tired and crabby after a long day at the Pentagon, plus all that commuting time.

About that time, my Pastor, Reverend Bob Rodeffer urged me "to get married to Bill, because he was a good man, who loved me and my kids too." I guess I knew we were serious about each other, for Bill had given up golfing on Sundays to go to Church with me instead! Still I had been fearful of marriage and being hurt again, it was hard to make "the big step."

In June 1957, Bill and I were married at our small Methodist Church. With Lew and Steve standing there beside us, plus two couples, Jean and Jess Greathouse and John and Virginia Catale, who were our best friends. Interestingly enough, they were all Catholics and had gotten special permission to attend our wedding. It was a "budget wedding," but we thought it was grand! Our honeymoon was a weekend at Ocean City, while Jean and Jess watched the boys for us.

We not only came back to work at the office, but we started working on a happy marriage. Bill was a disciplinarian and expected military-type obedience when he spoke. It was quite an adjustment for the boys, and for me.

Bill showed so much genuine love and gave generously of himself, to teach the boys and do things with them. He coached their base-ball, and football and bowling teams...it seems we'd just get over one athletic schedule and they'd be into another! We ate many late night sandwiches, trying to support their games. I didn't understand all the rules, but I was right out there cheering with all the other parents for "our Coach" and the "Witt" boys.

The love, the time and the discipline paid off. The boys never gave us a minutes worry. We always knew where they were, because we were with them, most of the time! After college, Lew and Steve each entered military service. Each of them told Bill, later, that they really appreciated his training at home, because it had prepared them for the respect of authority and discipline needed for a successful career. They might not have liked it at the time, but they appre-ciated it later. Me, too.

Bill and I were both active in church. It seemed like I couldn't say no and if the Pastor needed anything, he called on me. I could have been called "Mrs. Church," at one time...for it got to the point where I was there almost nightly for meetings. We felt we were "good Christians"...that was until my sister, Hazel, and her four children came to live with us while Art was sent to Thailand and Vietnam. They had two children since we had last seen them; Marty, born in Japan and baby Artie, Jr., born in California.

The little baby boy had died suddenly, when he was only five months old. They called it "crib death." Bill took care of our family, while I flew out to California for the funeral...it was so sad. I cried more than they did at the funeral. The organist played hymns I had come to love, but they were no comfort to me. As we left the cemetary with that tiny casket behind us, I really broke down with grief, and although Hazel and Art were crying, they were consoling me!

"How will you ever be able to move to another place and leave your baby here?" I asked.

"He's not here, Neet," Hazel said, with her arms around me. "Little Artie is with Jesus. Only a little body is left here, but he has gone to be with Jesus. I won't come back here, I don't need to." They had a confidence in that, which I didn't have. They were able to handle this death, knowing a peace, which really passed my under-standing. I returned home still grieving over it.

Hazel got pregnant as soon as possible after Artie's death and Jodi Lee was added to the family. When Hazel and the four little girls came to stay with us, we had quite a house full! We fell in love with those darling little girls and looked forward to being with my family after such a long separation.

9

Glenne and Lisa were about the same ages as Lew and Steve and they picked right up in their happy relationships and got along great. That left the two youngest, Marty and little Jodi, to amuse each other and they really did. It was fun to have girls, for a change, after just boys for so many years. We had to adjust to "curlers" and "frilly things" around.

We thought God was so good to give us this time to be together...we just did not know how good!

Hazel was different. It seemed all she wanted to do was read the Bible and talk about Jesus. But she was so jolly all the time, we loved her in spite of that!

Until that time, we didn't have a Bible in the house; except a lovely big Family Bible, that we never opened. We wondered what she could find so interesting in it, to read it every day! She told us that she and Art had given their hearts to Jesus while they were stationed in Japan. We thought that was nice, but didn't know what she was talking about! We'd never heard that expression in our Church.

Hazel jumped into helping at Church. Our new Methodist Pastor, Reverend "Mac" needed a Secretary and Hazel volunteered. She refused any pay..."I'm doing this for Jesus," she'd say. Hazel never grumbled nor complained, no matter how much anyone asked her to do. She helped the janitor and anyone else who needed a hand.

Hazel taught Sunday School and took on the teenagers. Since Lew and Steve were both in that age group, we were delighted. They had been wanting to get out of going to Sunday School, but Bill wouldn't discuss it.

"You will go, while you live at home," he told them firmly, and the matter was settled. Still, I was happy, because I knew they'd like being with Aunt Hazel. They did. She insisted everyone bring Bibles and they really had to study, for she challenged them. Those disinterested boys responded to her jolly nature and love of God's Word.

Soon Lew and Steve were singing in the choir, no small miracle! Along with Glenne and Lisa and some other teens they formed a senior high choir, for the first time, in our Church. Before long they were reading their Bibles and talking about Jesus! Just like Hazel they were telling us that our "church work" wouldn't get us into heaven! Boy! Did that make me mad! I was on the Official Board and Chairman of Evangelism...can you believe it? I didn't know what they were talking about??

Reverend "Mac" had started Sunday night services when he came to our Church, and Hazel never missed attending. The kids even liked it and would come home and tell us what we'd missed. Finally, I started going occasionally, just to keep them from asking me.

On May 5, 1967, we had a visiting Pastor speak that Sunday evening. He read from Matthew 7:21 "not everyone who says Lord, Lord will enter the Kingdom of heaven." He said that if we taught Sunday School, and went to church faithfully and worked there every night, when we died we wouldn't go to heaven unless we had met God's conditions to get in!

10

I didn't even know God had any conditions, so I wanted to hear more.

He read from Romans 10:9-10. It said that we must believe that Jesus was God's Son and that He had died and paid the penalty for our forgiveness of sins. We must confess this with our mouths, before people, publicly, or we could not be saved and go to heaven.

It was like a slap in the face! It hit me hard. I realized suddenly, that I had never really believed that Jesus was more than a good teacher and example. I said a little prayer acknowledging that Jesus was the Son of God and that He died for me and was raised up from the dead, and seated at the right hand of God. The Pastor had an altar call, and asked those to come up, who did this for the first time...they needed to make this confession publicly. I went up. I was crying so hard, I don't know if anyone else went up or not. But kneeling there, at the altar rail, I knew I was going to heaven! I had met God's conditions, at last, and I was so happy! I had that wonderful assurance and nothing since that time has ever made me doubt, because God's Word said it and I believed it. I was 40 years old, and life began to be "new" and exciting for me, from then on.

Immediately I had a desire to read the Bible! I figured if God had these "conditions," that I didn't know about....He might have lots of other things, that I needed to know about too. He did.

I went out and bought a Bible, on Monday, and began to read it, a little each evening before bedtime. But I was too sleepy and didn't get much out of it, so I decided to get up early to read the Bible. Bill said, "just be quiet and don't wake me when you get up," when I asked if it would be all right.

My first morning, I got up 15 minutes early, but by the time I washed my face and tiptoed into the kitchen, my time was almost up! So I knew that wouldn't work at all.

The next day, I got up a half an hour early, and started in Matthew, reading verse-by-verse. I found it was exciting! I soon changed to 45 minutes, and then I realized that I needed time to pray about some family problems, so I made it an hour. I had never really prayed before and God answered my prayer, the very first day I prayed! I was thrilled that God heard me, when I hardly knew Him at all. I began to look forward to that early hour, as the best part of my day. I still do.

I began to see things, in the Bible, I didn't understand, like Mark 16:16. Jesus said, "those who believe and are baptized shall be saved." I knew I had been sprinkled, as a child, but I wasn't a "believer" then. I asked my Pastor, Reverend "Mac," about it. He said I didn't need it, since I was baptized already. But I felt that Jesus had been baptized, in a river, and I'd like that too. So I just prayed about it and asked God to work it out, somehow -- if He wanted me to be baptized. He did. In June 1968, I was baptized, by a small church group, in a river, near Oakland, Maryland. What a blessing, as my husband and youngest son, Steve, saw me "buried and raised," according to Romans 6:3-6.

As I continued to read my Bible, I was blessed by reading the miracles that occured in the book of Acts. I wished we had that in our own church! When I got into I Corinthians Chapter 12, I didn't understand it at all. The "gifts" of the Spirit had never been mentioned in all my years in church. Again, I went to my Pastor. He was a precious man who loved the Bible and the Lord Jesus, but he felt that none of these gifts were for us today. Just for the apostles and disciples, at Pentecost.

I continued to read my Bible, but when I read I Corinthians 14, I quit. I read all about why and how these gifts were to be used, to edify the church, and the people. I got so frustrated, I just closed the Bible and began to pray. I told the Lord that I was wasting my time, to keep reading a book that wasn't for today. If any of these things were real and if the nine spiritual gifts were something for me, then I wanted to meet people who had these gifts. I wanted to know it wasn't fake. I wanted to know the truth.

That was on Friday morning. It was a long holiday weekend and we headed for our cabin, in western Maryland. PTL...that weekend changed my life!

As we neared our cabin we happened to meet Bud and Wilma Friend, coming down to the main road as we headed onto the narrow dirt road leading up the rugged Backbone Mountain. Bud and Wilma lived at the bottom of the mountain. Our cabin is located over the crest of it. They invited us to a picnic on Saturday afternoon. I had never met either of them before, though Bill had met Bud while hunting. I didn't want to go on a picnic! I had work to do. We chatted a few minutes with them and then we went on to our place.

On Saturday Bud drove over in his jeep to see us and begged us to come to the picnic. I was busy painting the kitchen and had lots to do. I was not interested in a picnic! We invited him in for coffee and he and Bill and I got acquainted. I kept painting, but tried to be polite. Somehow the discussion got to church. We asked where they attended and Bud said an "independent, non-denominational" church. I asked what they believed? Bud replied, "the Bible. We don't use any other literature, even in Sunday Schools, just the Bible." I was interested!

I asked if they believed all the Bible? He said, "Yes." So I threw him a bombshell and asked if they believed I Corinthians 12? When he said "yes" to that, I almost fell over! I could hardly believe it. I asked if they spoke in tongues and prophesied?

"Yes," was Bud's reply, "some do." Well, we talked about two hours! Then we went to the picnic!

I couldn't wait to meet the rest of those folks!

They were just ordinary people. I guess I expected spiritual giants. The food was good and I found the people friendly. They invited us to a home prayer meeting that night. Naturally I wanted to go, but wasn't sure that Bill would, so I left it to the Lord. If He wanted us to go, then Bill would want to go...and he did!

What a prayer meeting! They sang hymns and shared testimonies of answered prayers, then they asked for prayer requests. Everyone kneeled on the floor to pray. They prayed aloud going around the room, praying in turn. As one person would pray for the prayer requests mentioned, I heard others praying softly in tongues! It was so beautiful and I began to cry. I cried during the whole meeting.

God had answered my prayer for truth!

After the prayers were finished, they put a chair in the center of the room. They asked if anyone had a need and wanted special prayer, they could sit in the chair. I jumped right in it.

I asked them to pray for me to receive all nine gifts of the spirit mentioned in I Corinthians 12. They laid hands on me and prayed. While I was still sitting in the chair and everyone gathered around me, their Pastor began to prophesy. I had never heard prophecy, but I knew what it was, from what I had read in the Bible.

It was most astounding! He said that we would have to leave our church. The people would not want us there! That was hard to believe, since we had gone to that church for about 15 years. Reverend Mac had been transferred and we had a new Pastor, but we loved everyone and they loved us. I knew if it were a message from God, it would come to pass. It did.

But that's another chapter in my life. An ordinary woman, who found a new life, eternal life, when she moved from Alaska to the Pentagon.

Chapter 3

PENTECOST COSTS YOU SOMETHING

What a picnic! What a prayer meeting! I could hardly wait to
tell Hazel what happened that weekend. We attended Bud and Wilma's
church, "Sunnyside Chapel," Sunday morning. I called Hazel long
distance to tell her the news that I had met people who spoke in
tongues and prophesied, and believed all the Bible! I told her about
having them pray for me to receive the Baptism in the Holy Spirit.
It was so fantastic it couldn't wait for our return home so I could
tell Hazel all the details I couldn't share over the telephone.

Hazel was excited as I was. It changed everything to know the
Bible was a whole book for believers today -- not just the early
apostles! Miracles, healings -- things our church needed were still
available, if we would believe and act. Right away, Hazel and I
wanted to go to the Full Gospel meetings Bud and Wilma and the other
Christians had recommended. We knew now there was more that God had
for us and we wanted it all.

Bill and Art weren't too keen on going to a meeting they knew
nothing about nor anyone present. But they did like to have dinner
out, so they agreed to go to the big S&W Cafeteria in Rockville,
Maryland, where a monthly Full Gospel Businessmen's Meeting was to be
held. None of us knew what to expect, but off we went to find the
cafeteria.

After the dinner people began to sing. Then there were prayer
request forms to fill out. The group of men at the head table prayed
over all the slips of paper. It sure was different. They laid hands
on each other, and put their free hands on the pile of papers, and
"agreed" in prayer. The prayer was full of faith and I wished I'd
have put more people on my prayer slip. I had a definite feeling
those prayers were going to be answered!

People were so happy and hugging others nearby. Most people
raised their hands high in the air when they sang. The leader said
it "pleased God" and read Psalms 63:3-4 and had us sing it. He asked
us to all lift our hands in worship as we sang. I felt so self-
conscious! I did lift one hand, about waist high. I saw Hazel lift

both hands high as her head. She was always one to tell me, "You have to be willing to be a fool for the Lord, if you want His blessings."

During the meeting we heard an exciting testimony by the guest speaker and the men liked it -- well enough to say we'd go back next month. That was too long to wait! It was Friday night and Hazel and I decided we'd go to "New Adventures in Prayer," on Monday night. We'd found some flyers at the dinner and thought we'd see what else was going on in the area we didn't know about. We discovered there were lots of things happening we didn't know about!

"NAIP" was packed -- quite unbelievable to us, for a midweek service! The song leader was Timmy Edwards and she got a little scripture song going and people were clapping their hands. It was just great to see people enjoying their religion! We were accustomed to a quiet church and everyone serious. We never heard such "gusto" singing and again happy people -- smiling and hugging each other.

Another song was sung and afterwards the people began to sing a spontaneous song all around us. We just listened -- we had never heard anything like it! It sounded like angels in Heaven -- the harmony was just beautiful. We could hear those near us and everyone was singing, but something different. How astounding! Some sang in tongues and others in English, words of praise to Jesus, the Lamb of God. It didn't bother us that people were singing different words, as they stood with their eyes closed and hands raised high.

It was the most beautiful singing we had ever heard! Yet, unplanned. It had to be the Holy Spirit -- no choir could have done it better with a director!

When it was finished, Hazel leaned over to me and said, "We should take off our shoes, we are on holy ground." We did. It was the first of many times we sat, without shoes, during a "New Adventures in Prayer" service. It was aptly named! It was indeed a new adventure for us -- and one we longed to share with our husbands.

The leader was a short, slim man and rather quiet. Everyone seemed to know him and made an effort to get over to hug Jack Zirkle. He kept everything on schedule during the meeting and invited people forward for prayer afterwards. We didn't dare stay out any longer, so Hazel and I headed home when the meeting ended. It was an exciting night and so much was new to us -- we could hardly wait till the next Monday night.

We had another new experience that first night at NAIP. After a very worshipful song, "He is Lord," was sung, a hush fell over the crowd. Someone spoke aloud briefly, in tongues, and then there came an interpretation. It was very encouraging, telling us "God was pleased with our praise and we should continue to worship Him." We then understood the Scripture that stated "tongues, with interpretation, would edify the Church."

We attended "New Adventures in Prayer" regularly and our faith grew. We had a hunger for more of Jesus in our lives as we heard how God used other people miraculously. I couldn't hear or read enough about what God was doing in the lives of people throughout the world.

In January 1969, Don Basham spoke at "New Adventures in Prayer." Afterward he had prayer and laying on of hands for those seeking the baptism in the Holy Spirit. My sister, Hazel, and I went forward. Art and Bill attended the meeting too, but they didn't want to go for the prayer so they waited for us. It took a long time to get these big "logs" burning, but we were like kindling and easily "caught fire."

Hazel received a beautiful language immediately and I was thrilled. But when he laid hands on me and prayed I only received a few syllables..."Alla-ma-da." That was all.

I was so disappointed, and felt I hadn't been given a prayer language. I didn't like the words at all. It was like baby talk and I just rejected it.

The next morning I decided to spend my time in prayer, instead of reading my Bible. So I knelt there in my kitchen and asked God to baptize me in the Holy Spirit. I reminded God that I had done everything in the Scriptures and I had nothing else to do, except speak. I told God I would say anything, any words that He would give me to say. Immediately the same words, "Alla-ma-da," came to mind. I began to speak them over and over and thank God for them. I knew these words were from God after all. If I had been making up words, I'd have picked something that sounded prettier!!

As I continued to use these words, God gave me more words to praise Him with, but each time it took faith to speak them out. They were unknown words to me and naturally I did not understand them. That is how faith is needed for this miracle to take place. The miracle isn't that we speak or use our voice. The miracle is the words the Holy Spirit gives us to speak.

Eight years later a friend heard my testimony and he received the interpretation for my very first words, the ones I had rejected. It was, "God is my Father." Praise the Lord! As yet, I have never had anyone recognize my prayer language to identify it as Rumanian or Portugese or any other known language. However, at one Full Gospel Businessmen's Fellowship International Convention in Washington, D.C., with thousands of people there, a black man I never saw before, stood to give a message in tongues. He spoke the same words the Lord had given me! What a blessing! To know that God gives the same language to more than one person was very reassuring. Yet I realized faith must be based entirely upon God's Word, not an experience. I'm glad mine was. But using my unknown prayer language was a big step of faith for me, and these two events were most encouraging and exciting.

At New Adventures in Prayer, we heard some beautiful and exciting testimonies. The one that thrilled us most was by a Methodist Minister, Derrel Emmerson. Derrel later became Pastor of a non-denominational Church, to which Bill and I belong, called "Christian Assembly." His testimony was of wanting more of God's Spirit and power in his life. What it cost him, in terms of misunderstanding and rejection, we could identify with completely!

We discovered there were meetings every night, somewhere in the Washington area. Our first inclination was to try to get to all of them! We heard for the first time that these people were called "charismatic." One thing we knew for sure -- they loved to praise the Lord. The meetings were so joyful and full of exciting testimonies, we wanted to be with these people.

Needless to say, our church seemed very dull in comparison. We had an elderly pastor by now, and the ritual we had once found very comfortable was now vain repetition. Hazel and I agreed it was no wonder people stayed away from church -- or nodded during the service. We longed to "liven up" our church, and I guess we were crusaders. When we would say an occasional "Amen" or "Praise the Lord," it definately was not appreciated. We kept praying for God to pour out His Spirit in our little church and into people that we loved.

We looked forward more and more to the Monday night meetings at NAIP and the FGBMFI monthly meetings, where we could see and hear more of the exciting things God was doing throughout the world, by the move of the Holy Spirit. It just wasn't happening in our church and no one there seemed to know we were missing anything. They were content with status quo, while we seemed to get more "hungry" all the time for spirit-baptized believers.

At New Adventures in Prayer one evening, we met some people who told us of a 6 a.m. Saturday morning prayer meeting out in our vicinity. We wanted to try it. It only lasted two hours and we thought we could be home before the family was hardly awake.

It was a small group, meeting in -- of all places -- a small Methodist Church! It was led by Navy Commander Bob Thomas and his wife, Cozette. As soon as we met them, they made us feel that we'd known them forever. They were just warm and friendly and the little prayer meeting was great. We were down on our knees praying before the sun came up.

What a beautiful way to begin your day!

We could see our Saturdays were too busy to get to this meeting very often. I knew Bill wouldn't stand for a 9:30 breakfast very much and when we got home, he was out cutting the grass "early" and a bit cranky at being neglected. So we decided that we had better skip that meeting.

Bob and Cozette learned that Hazel and I lived near Davidsonville and invited us to a home meeting that they attended regularly and enjoyed, which met on Wednesday evenings. They gave us directions. It sounded like what we had been looking for...a prayer group close to home!

Wednesday night came and we had asked our husbands to come along, but neither Bill nor Art cared to go. Off we went to find the home of Navy Lieutenant Commander Bob Wright in Davidsonville, Maryland. We didn't have any trouble. Lots of cars surrounded his driveway. We were a bit timid to ring the doorbell at a strangers' home, but we had come this far and couldn't turn back now.

We rang the doorbell and waited for a new adventure. We were greeted with hugs and introduced ourselves -- we'd never remember anyone in that large crowd! People were everywhere -- kitchen, living and dining rooms. Handsome Midshipmen and lots of young people were a bit of a surprise to us, because we know how hard it is to get the younger folks to attend church, much less a prayer group.

17

Bob and Cozette Thomas spotted us and came to welcome us and soon the meeting got underway. Cozette played a musical instrument, an autoharp. I'd never seen one before. I really admired her playing it, as she taught us all a "new" Scripture song. Little did I dream I would be learning to play an autoharp by the year's end. Before Bob and Cozette left for Japan, to serve as missionaries, Cozette helped me tune my new autoharp. She gave me a few cards, containing the words and the chords, so I could learn to play scripture songs. I've been playing the autoharp ever since. It was a great meeting -- Bible study, praise, prayer, testimonies. No one wanted to leave, but Bob Wright ran a tight ship and got the "Mids" away on time.

The next week Bill and Art agreed to join Hazel and I. Bill said he would go "just once," but if he didn't like it, I wasn't to ask him again. We prayed all week that Bill and Art would love it as much as we did. They definitely were in for a different kind of prayer meeting. The difference began at the front door!!

When we walked in, we were greeted with the usual friendly hugs -- this was not "usual" for our men however. Bill was stiff as a board, and I could see he didn't want anymore of that! But it seemed every male in the place got to him! Later he sat with folded arms and simply observed throughout the entire evening.

Art was doing about the same. Even though they both liked to sing, they didn't know these new Scripture songs, so they couldn't join in -- if they had wanted to. I wasn't sure they wanted to!

The meeting was great and we drove home expecting the men had enjoyed it, too.

"I'm never going back," Bill announced, "I don't like being hugged by men! It's ridiculous."

"They were just being friendly," I reasoned with him. But his jaw was set and I knew the discussion was ended.

The following Wednesday, I asked Bill if he wouldn't reconsider and come with us to the meeting. Art agreed to go -- if Bill would.

"All right, but on one condition. Don't let any of those men hug me," he replied.

"How could I stop them, honey?" I asked. I knew there was no way I could prevent it.

"You just walk ahead of me and tell them, or I won't go," he told me firmly.

"I'll try," was all I could say. And I did -- but it didn't work.

Everyone hugged him! But they were so friendly, he felt more at ease. He could see they weren't "weirdos."

He and Art liked the fact there were lots of men attending the meeting. There were more men than women, which was completely opposite in our Church. He and Art enjoyed the "new kinds of songs" and soon joined right in.

One evening we were all in for a treat, when two visiting evangelists from Chard, England, came to the meeting. They had visited before, we learned, when traveling in the USA, and everyone eagerly awaited their ministry. Tony Nash and Vick Dunning astounded us playing tambourines. We had never heard anything like it! Not loud, but skillfully keeping time to the music. It added so much to the other instruments. We loved it! Both men, Tony and Vick, shared what the Lord was doing in Europe through the outpouring of the Holy Spirit.

This "Church," meeting in a home, was feeding us spiritually much more than our own traditional Church where we'd been members for 15 years. It was so regulated, by programs and ritual, the Holy Spirit couldn't move very much if He had tried! We loved the people and wanted them to know about the Holy Spirit and exciting things the Lord was doing...but it seemed no one wanted to hear. We worked hard supporting the Church. We were active in everything and encouraging more prayer and Bible study. People didn't seem interested. In fact, it seemed they moved away from us, literally. If we came in and sat on one side, the other members would sit on the opposite!

The only thing we could see that we were doing differently was that we carried our Bibles, and looked up Scriptures when they were quoted...and of course we said "Praise the Lord" and "Amen." It made us different.

The rejection we experienced really hurt. We finally gave up, and withdrew our membership, It was hard to do, but God helped us. Not one person ever called or came to see us. We thought we had a lot of friends, but no one missed us enough to call and tell us. No one invited us over for a meal or evening visit. That really hurt.

Looking back now, I can see that if anyone had begged us to stay on in the Church, we'd have probably stayed. If friends had called, it would have been too difficult to leave. This way it was easy. So we moved on to join others, who had left traditional Churches for more of the Spirit of God in their lives. I heard it said "Pentecost costs you something"...and it surely was true!

We loved the new friends and freedom of worship, in the home meetings. We enjoyed meeting visitors and Pastors, from the charismatic Church in South Chard, England who came occasionally to Lieutenant Commander Bob Wright's home meetings, and shared from the Word. They always brought some new Scripture songs for us to learn and we loved having a new song to sing unto the Lord.

Many of us longed to go and visit this exciting, spiritually-blessed Church in England. Many did go to visit "Uncle Sid," their Pastor, and his wife, "Auntie Mill"...but that is another story.

Chapter 4

THE BIG LOG BURNS

Bill and Art continued attending the prayer meetings on Wednesday nights in Bob Wright's home for three years. Both of them really enjoyed it, but they never asked for prayer to receive the baptism in the Holy Spirit. It was very obvious they were the only two in the group who needed this blessing. During this time Hazel and I had been praying for our husbands to experience more spiritual growth. Finally God began to work on my heart, that I should stop going to any meetings without my husband.

"Lord," I prayed, "I really want my husband to be the leader of our home, but he just doesn't seem interested in growing spiritually. I'm so miserable. The way life is right now, I can't share lots of wonderful spiritual blessings with him. You know, Lord, he scoffs or ridicules when I tell him about some of the miracles that happen."

I continued pouring out my heart to God, "You know I love him Lord. I want Bill to enjoy spiritual things -- but I'm getting tired of begging him to go places with me. Lord, I never read in the Bible where a woman had to push her husband. They were leaders. I want Bill to lead, too." I concluded, "I just don't know what to do."

God spoke in my ear, "Stop leading -- so your husband can."

I was amazed at how simple God's solution was to my problems! But I didn't see "how" it could work -- soon anyway. I was so discouraged over his lack of interest in spiritual things, I decided to try what God had said. Even though it didn't seem like it could help.

I called Hazel and told her, "I am not going to any more meetings -- unless Bill wants to go. I am not going to Church or anywhere until God changes his heart and he begins to be the spiritual leader in our home." I was pretty sad when I told her my decision -- I could envision myself never going anywhere, ever again.

"You really need fellowship," Hazel told me, "you ought to go to church at least."

"No, my mind is made up -- I can't go on like this," I replied. "If I can't share everything with Bill -- the person who is closest to my heart -- then I don't want any more blessings."

I shed a lot of tears, thinking of all I was giving up. God had a surprise in store for me, however. After dinner, that very night, Bill and I sat down to talk and hrson who is closest to my heart -- then I don't want any more blessings."

I shed a lot of tears, thinking of all I was giving up. God had a surprise in store for me, however. After dinner, that very night, Bill and I sat down to talk a   Then this big, strong husband of mine began to cry! Bill never cried, except twice in all our married life, when his Dad and Mother had died. He was not an emotional person. So I realized this was serious.

They had him pushed out of a position he had held for two years, while they reorganized. He'd been so capable and the promotion was assured him during the entire reorganization. Now, suddenly, an outsider was brought in for the position and he was told he didn't "qualify." It didn't make sense that he was qualified for two years, but now he wasn't. The job had been rewritten and upgraded. The people who worked for Bill were upset, too, but there was nothing anyone could do. He would have to train the new man and move back to his former office.

"I don't know why God allowed this to happen to me," Bill said, through tears of frustration.

"I know why," I replied.

"Honey, the Bible says if you put God first in your life -- all things will be added to you." I gulped, but finished making my point. "And you aren't doing that."

"What do you mean?" Bill's voice began to rise, "I'm a better Christian than most men. I go to church every Sunday!"

I know you do," I replied. I was sorry I had said anything, but it was too late now. I continued, "But you don't read the Bible and it is God's love letters to you. He's your best friend and you won't read His letters and you won't pray and talk to Him. How can you expect Him to bless you if you won't even talk to Him?

"I go to church and we give a lot of money, and time, helping out" -- he snapped his reply.

I had to agree. "Yes, you go to church faithfully, but you get angry if the Pastor is five minutes overtime. You get all upset, because you'll be late for the football game!" Though it was true, I was on a touchy subject. "You lose any blessing you might have gotten during church."

"All right," Bill said, "I want you to get me up in the mornings and I'm going to start reading the Bible when you do. And I'm going to start going to prayer meetings. Everything you do, I'm going to do," he said. I could hardly believe my ears!

"And," Bill continued, "if God doesn't change things in six months -- I'm not going to go any more!" It was an ultimatum. "Honey," I told him, "you can't talk that way to God! You can't give Him a deadline."

"Well," Bill answered, and his voice had a finality to it, "If He can't do it in six months, He can't do it at all."

"God can do more than you could ever ask, and if you do put Him first in your life -- He'll get your job back for you," I replied.

"I wish I was as confident as you," he told me and gave me a hug.

True to his word, Bill started getting up in the mornings and began to read his Bible. I was in my usual spot, in the kitchen, and he preferred his living room easy chair.

I prayed so fervently for God to honor Bill's commitment and bless him. It did seem impossible to change the situation, but the Bible said "nothing is impossible with God." I believed it -- no matter how it looked.

I kept my word too -- I didn't push Bill into going to meetings or church programs. I would tell him about speakers, etc., but if he said "no," that was it. I felt if there was a speaker or meeting I was supposed to attend -- Bill would want to go. I had real peace about my decision and never felt "bad" about the meetings I missed -- because Bill and I went together now. Not as much as I'd have chosen, but I was so happy to have him go willingly, I never complained.

It was soon apparent to me that Bill was making the decisions -- not me! He was leading at last! At last we could talk abut everything -- what an answer to prayer! And God had answered the very day I prayed! I never had to miss Church or Wednesday night prayer meeting. I gave up everything, but God gave me back every bit -- and more.

Meanwhile, a couple of weeks had gone by and Bill came home pretty discouraged at night. I dreaded asking "how things were going" -- it was really difficult for him to be demoted. "Nothing's changed," was about all he'd say. I kept praying and encouraged Bill to pray. "I am," he told me.

"But Honey, there is a lot of power when two, or more, pray together." I urged him to pray aloud with me. It was difficult at first, his prayers were so brief and he was self-conscious. I just rejoiced that he was resisting the devil, who wouldn't ever have us pray, by praying with me.

God answered our prayers for Bill's job in a most miraculous way.

"Mr. J. resigned today," Bill told me on the way home. "He what? He just started three weeks ago! What happened?" I couldn't believe what I was hearing.

"He just told the big boss he was going to leave the area and had accepted another job. He's leaving next week!"

"Oh, honey," I said, "that's great! Now the Lord can give you the job again."

"I don't think so -- they rewrote the job description and without a college degree I don't think I can qualify."

Sure enough, that's what they told him. He'd never get the job again. He couldn't qualify. Now Bill was really discouraged!

"God is going to give you that job," I assured him, "because you are putting Him first. Don't give up."

We prayed harder than ever.

Two weeks passed. Mr. J. had gone and Bill was back up front "filling in," as he had done for two years prior to all this. Only now it was temporary, until they could fill the job with someone else -- someone who could qualify.

They tried. But no one qualified. Finally a special review panel was convened and their decision was to rewrite the job and give it to the man who had proven his capability. My husband!

Six weeks after Bill had given God the proper place in his life -- God had turned the situation around, in a most remarkable way. Bill had given God six months to prove His word and He had done it in six weeks!

This miraculous answer to prayer really boosted our faith and Bill has never missed a morning of rising early to study the Bible. He has never skipped a prayer meeting or church -- he is determined to keep God first in his priorities.

Not long after this happened, we invited Hazel and Art to come and join us for dinner and an evening of very special fellowship. We had invited a visiting minister from Chard, England, Brother Andrew Jordan and his wife, Joy, and daughter Elizabeth, to our home for dinner. They were in the USA for a month, sharing, teaching and blessing everyone at the New Covenant Church, meeting now in Tommy Parlett's basement.

More than a hundred people came on Sunday afternoons to the New Covenant Church in Annapolis. What glorious meetings they were! Often lasting 3-4 hours. Our friend, Emma Aiello, always went with us and she loved it too.

While the men were outdoors keeping an eye on the barbeque grill and its sizzling contents, we ladies had time to talk, as we put finishing touches on the meal. We expressed our desire for our men to move into the spiritual gifts and the baptism in the Holy Spirit. We couldn't understand their reluctance.

"God has given each of us just what we need," Joy assured us. "We women are so quick to move into spiritual things. We hear of a blessing and we want it immediately, and we rush off to get in on it." We laughed -- that was surely true! Joy continued, "But God has given us our husbands, who aren't like that at all. They must analyze and consider everything, so carefully, before they make a move. Even when they finally decide it's scripturally good and they desire it, often they still wait a year just "thinking it over."

"God has planned it that way," Joy said. "Do you see? It's for our protection. They keep us from getting off into a lot of deception and kooky stuff."

We agreed with her logic, and Joy concluded, "those husbands of yours are like big old logs -- and you girls are like kindling. God had to get you burning first and will use you to get those logs on fire. A big log doesn't start burning easily, but when they do, they last a long time and give off more heat than the kindling ever could. Get ready for those logs to catch on."

We all had a good laugh over this comparison of our men and big old logs.

It was perhaps another year before Bill received the baptism in the Holy Spirit. It came about when we attended Tennessee-Georgia Christian Camp in 1972. Bill went forward for prayer, after a teaching on the subject by Rev. Don Basham. He received immediately. His language sounded like an African dialect. Bill had the unique experience of speaking in two different languages in one day. I heard it and was so astounded.

That night in the worship service, prior to the evening speaker, Bill sang in the Spirit for the first time. This time his "new tongue" sounded like Chinese. I thought of those few halting words I had received and my struggle to have freedom to use my new prayer language. What a difference it was for Bill! The new tongue was no problem at all -- the words just poured forth effortlessly. It thrilled my heart to see him move into the gift of the Holy Spirit, at last. He told me later, he had wanted the baptism for over a year, but wouldn't humble himself and ask for prayer. His pride got in his way.

The "big log" had caught fire, at last, and has burned brightly ever since!!

Chapter 5

THE PENTAGON

The Pentagon building, which houses most of the headquarters personnel of the Department of Defense, is virtually a city in itself. The five-sided, five-storied building occupies 34 acres near the Potomac River, opposite the Nation's capital, in Arlington, Virginia.

The original site of the building was little more than wasteland, swamp, and rendering works known as "Hell's Bottom." According to a 1966 Department of Defense brochure, "into this waste, 5 1/2 million cubic yards of earth were poured, and 41,492 concrete piles were hammered into place. Then on this man-made mound, 600,000 tons of sand and gravel, dredged from the Potomac River, were processed into 435,000 cubic yards of concrete and molded into the Pentagon form."

The building has three times the office space of the 102-floor Empire State Building in New York. Five U.S. Capitol buildings, could neatly fit within the walls of the Pentagon with room to spare, so we are told. The fortress-like shape makes the building unique. With only five floors, the height is small. The proximity to National Airport necessitated that it not be so high as to pose a hazard to planes taking off and landing at this busy airport.

Each of the five outside walls is 921 feet in length, so the distance around the outermost ring of the building is almost a mile! There are 17 1/2 miles of corridors. The mile around perimeter wall is faced with Indiana limestone. On the two sides of the building facing Washington are two main entrances, the River and the Mall. The River Entrance faces an attractive lagoon. This lagoon provides access by water, to the Pentagon, and mooring for small craft.

A unique feature of the building is the access to offices provided by wide ramps between floors. These ramps would be particularly useful in case of emergencies, when it might be necessary to clear the thousands of workers rapidly. These ramps may be efficient, but they are hard on your feet! Sore feet are the common characteristic of the Pentagon employee. Besides the ramps, there are 150 stairways, 19 escalators and 13 elevators for freight, or handicapped persons.

The Pentagon was designed and built in a race against time, and was planned for efficiency, not beauty. Frills and non-functional items were omitted wherever possible. Passenger elevator service was eliminated due to wartime economy.

Construction began on September 11, 1941, on a 24-hour a day schedule. At one stage, fifteen thousand men were employed on the job. Work was completed at record speed. The first office workers began to move in on April 29, 1942. All construction was completed by January 15, 1943. Under normal conditions, construction of such a building would take four years. In spite of the speed with which the building was erected, the Pentagon has held up well.

At wartime peak, about 33,000 employees worked in the Pentagon in three shifts. After World War II, speculation about what the building could be used for was a favorite lunchtime topic. There was talk, in 1946, of converting the building into a hospital for veterans. Unless there is a change in the mood of the world, the Pentagon will never be too big or unnecessary.

With unification of the armed services in 1947, the Pentagon became headquarters for the entire military. Originally designated as the National Military Establishment, it later became the Department of Defense. In January 1954, the Pentagon housed 29,000 military and civilian employees.

There are large floor plans posted on the walls and postcard size floor plans are available at the Information Desks. It is well organized and well planned. The floor plan is identical for all five floors and the basement. Moreover, each floor is painted a different color and large signs are posted over doorways, corridors and rings. The office numbering system is designed to identify the office by floor, ring and corridor. With a little experience, it becomes very easy to find any given destination. Despite the vastness of the Pentagon, no two offices are more than 1,800 feet apart -- for the hardy and experienced employee about a ten minute walk. The Pentagon is perhaps one of the most talked about public buildings in the world. The jokes about the vast building have remained popular with passage of time. Everyone has heard about the wartime Western Union boy who went there to deliver a telegram and came out a week later as a full Colonel.

There are daily conducted tours for visitors starting from the Concourse. Otherwise, only the concourse area is open to the public, unless escorted by an employee. For the visitor, there are a number of points of interest within the Pentagon. The walls of many corridors display a collection of paintings, engravings, etchings, and photographs by combat artists and photographers. Throughout the building there are large models of Navy vessels and Air Force planes and missiles.

Occasionally you will see such items as trophies, flags and battle relics. Special attention is given to the Hall of Heroes, where every Medal of Honor recipient is listed, and there are displays of the medals.

Because of its isolated location, the Pentagon operates a little

26

city within its walls. Shopping facilities, available on the 135 x 690 foot concourse, are comparable to those of a fair sized mall. There is a uniform and clothing store, a branch of a local department store, candy counter, a large bookstore, a greeting card shop, a bakery, a shoe repair, cleaners, drug store, men's shoe store, an optometrist, ladies hosiery and boutique, a florist, a jewelry store, a newsstand, a post office, a Government Printing Office sales store, a credit union, bank and barber shop. People get sick at the Pentagon, but there are facilities for military and civilian emergencies.

All agencies are served by the vast Army Library. It contains over 300,000 volumes and periodicals in all languages.

With the completion of the metro station, most of the traffic in and out of the Pentagon is far below the building or at the bus terminal outside. The old bus lanes are still used by taxi's, official Department of Defense buses, chartered buses and vanpools, picking up or discharging passengers. The government encourages vanpools and carpools. There are acres of parking areas adjacent to the building. Except for "visitors parking" area, every parking area is assigned. The closest to the building are designated for handicapped and vanpools or carpools. Further out goes to those carpools with fewer than four members. Special Police check permits and give tickets to the frustrated motorists who don't have a sticker, or to those who get called in at odd hours and hurriedly park anywhere and fail to move out, before the police start checking.

There are many signs, but no traffic lights, and very few policemen. If a driver misses or ignores a direction sign, he gets into trouble. If drivers obey the signs, it works perfectly. At the height of rush hours, busses, cars, and pedestrians stream into the area peacefully. With the completion of the underground Metro system, providing fast rail service to the Pentagon, the congestion of buses has lessened.

The Pentagon Police are on duty 24-hours a day. The guards are trained in fire fighting and there is fire equipment on hand for immediate use. There has never been a murder in the Pentagon, we've been told. There have been several births, and deaths from natural causes.

The Pentagon Police have much work with demonstrators, as well as dignitaries coming and going at the entrances, and there are thefts within the building, but cars are the favorite target. In addition to the police, there are military guards in certain areas and a group of security-intelligence personnel who protect internal security matters.

Keeping the Pentagon clean is no small task. There are 83 acres of offices, and 107 acres of floors to be cleaned. Most of this cleaning is done at night. In the 280 restrooms, 175,000 rolls of toilet paper, 35 million paper towels and 12,500 quarts of liquid soap were used in one year. More than seven acres of glass in 7,748 windows must be cleaned. Because of budget cuts the building no longer gets painted every seven years. Some offices have waited more than 10 years, and it shows.

Where to go for lunch? Pentagon people have several choices. Cafeterias, snack bars, or the 5-acre center court (when the weather is warm), which provides a park-like atmosphere for those who like eating lunch in the sunshine. There are occasional events held in the center court, to lighten a hectic day, such as concerts by military bands or a savings bond rally, complete with such famous people as Miss America. There are award ceremonies and rare visits by the President. Celebrities such as Billy Graham conduct religious services in the Auditorium or outdoors. Noon hour is also the busiest time of day at the Pentagon Officers Athletic Center, a popular health club, underground, that offers members racquetball, swimming, handball, squash, a complete exercise room or jogging to trim the waistline.

This concludes our brief tour of the Pentagon. I hope you can come here someday and see it for yourself. Come along with me now and meet some of the real people who work in this city called the Pentagon.

Chapter 6

WHAT IS A MEDITATION ROOM?

When people hear that there is a Meditation Room in the Pentagon, this question comes forth, "What is a Meditation Room?"

It is a room used for quiet meditation by those working in the building. The room is available for non-denominational Bible studies and prayer groups, which are sponsored by the Military District of Washington Chaplains, who control the use of the room. Actually, there are two rooms in one. As you come into the room from the main corridor, there is one room marked "Group Meditation" and another "Private Meditation." The group room has a door, which is closed when in use.

There is a quiet hush when you enter. The wall-to-wall carpet helps soothe the noise, rather like a chapel. The lighting is dim in the room marked "Private," and there are a dozen large comfortable chairs. The chairs face a large fake stained glass window, lit from behind, which gives the room a soft light.

People come and go. It is a quiet place, to get away from pressures of the job, during the lunch hour or a coffee break. It seems like the only quiet place in the whole building, an "oasis of calm," from the turmoil of ringing phones and clacking typewriters.

Ask people about the Meditation Room and some will tell you "it's a place to rest," or "it is a room to get away from it all," or "it really does something for me." Some say, "I come here for a little peace and quiet, or "in bad weather this room is crowded...they should have one on every floor."

In the "group" room, there are 20 chairs around the walls and a coffee table in the center of the room, even though there is no eating or drinking allowed. The table usually contains some monthly publications, such as "Guideposts" or "Voice" magazines, which will provide uplifting reading for anyone with only a few minutes to rest. The "group" room also has a lighted panel, which resembles a stained glass window. This room is well lighted, for use by small Bible study groups. The room is used daily, at noon, by the ladies' Bible study and prayer groups. There are similar groups for men, who meet at different lunch times, and all are delighted the room is available for the non-denominational meetings. Attendance has grown and the small room is filled with people, sitting on the floor, standing along the walls, as well as every chair that can be squeezed in. And still people come! They come with their problems, their needs, and with joys to share. They leave refreshed and encouraged.

Former Secretary of Defense Melvin Laird noted that the room "is a place where men and women can reflect and pray and find guidance and inspiration." If one does not care to pray, the room is a good place to sit, relax and gather ones' thoughts, in peace and quiet. The Meditation Room serves as a retreat to men and women of the Pentagon.

Chapter 7

PENTAGON COMPLETED

Until December 15, 1970, the fellowship of Christians was carried on at lunchtime or prior to working hours, in tiny offices, unused conference rooms, the cafeteria, a bench, or on the grass in the center courtyard. Often these meetings were "bumped" out of rooms if they were needed for official use. Still the groups persevered and grew.

Secretary of Defense Melvin Laird felt the Pentagon was not complete without a place for people to pray and meditate, if they so desired, and the room was created out of an existing hallway. It was miraculous! Two small rooms were designed to utilize floor space that had been thought unusable -- but God used it and something wonderful came from nothing!

Secretary Laird, a former Representative in the Congress, was familiar with such a room, since it was in 1955 that Congress built its meditation room, under the Rotunda of the Capitol building. On December 15, 1970, hundreds of employees and dignitaries gathered for dedication ceremonies.

On the day of the dedication of the Pentagon Meditation Room, Secretary Laird said, "In a sense, this ceremony marks the completion of the Pentagon, for until now this building lacked a place where man's inner spirit could find expression." The Secretary of Defense reminded the audience that the Pentagon has most facilities to satisfy the needs of the body. "In the Concourse and corridors of this building can be found a wide range of goods and services of a material nature as well as places for work and duty. Today, we are dedicating a room in the Pentagon as a place where the needs of the spirit -- the needs of the inner man -- can find satisfaction. It is a place where men and women can reflect and pray and find guidance as well as inspiration."

Secretary Laird continued, "The room offers a setting in which we can pray as we like. Its existence is a recognition of our dependence on God if we are to progress toward the peace which we

31

seek for ourselves and for all mankind. Peace is the business of this building -- this small room is an affirmation of that.

"Though we cling to the principle that church and state should be separate, we do not propose to separate man from God. For without Him, Who is the source of our being, the source of our wisdom, and the source of our strength, we can do nothing," Secretary Laird said.

The ceremonies began with the invocation by John C. Broger, Director of Information for the Armed Forces, followed by Chaplain (Col) Hans E. Sandrock, USAF, and Chaplain (MG) Francis L. Sampson, USA, conducting the ceremony.

It was a brief ceremony, but a highlight in the lives of many people who had longed for a place, in that vast building, where they could gather consistently -- to pray or to read the Bible. At last we had a home!

The Pentagon was completed!

Chapter 8

EVERYBODY HAS TO EAT

Noon! Lunchtime in the Pentagon goes fast, it seems, for it takes six to ten minutes to get from various offices to the cafeterias or the big shopping area, called the "Concourse." To cut down on congestion in these areas, the serving time is from 11 a.m. to 2 p.m., in the many large cafeterias. People are drawn by the mixed aromas...of spicy pizza, french fries, 'burgers, tacos, or the ever present diet foods, served in the "PIK-QUIK," fast food cafeteria.

The building is a beehive of activity during lunchtime...people on errands, dashing into the shops, the whole Concourse is crowded. Outside, sweaty joggers are keeping fit. The required Fitness Tests keep everyone weight conscious, and hundreds of men and women use their lunchtime to run. Rainy, hot, typically humid summers, or snow,...whatever the season, they are always out there!

An outsider might think "no one could possibly be working, with all this activity going on," but with 25,000 people working in one building, the crowds you see at any one time, are just a tiny tip of an iceberg of humanity!

The Pentagon doesn't close down and take a siesta at noon. Though everyone has to eat, and everyone does get a lunch period, there are alert people on duty, 24 hours a day.

There are vital functions which are on-going, in the wee hours of the nights, holidays, year-round. People who perform these duties are the unsung heros guarding our Nation by manning desks, phones and computers, ever prepared and ready to defend and maintain our peace. Our Pentagon people never seem to be noticed; except in time of crisis! Still, a spirit of dedication and patriotism is the driving force amongst the military and civilians working there.

Everybody does have to eat...everybody does get a lunchtime; but not everyone uses the time to eat. There are a few employees, who would much prefer a "spiritual break" and food from God's Word, rather than physical food. To this tiny group of people, the lunchtime has become the highlight of their day. Compared to the 25,000 employees in this building...this is a tiny fragment who have chosen to give their lunchtime to God. Though there are many things that lure and entice them to use their lunchtime for other activities...there are some men and women who have found "food, that the world knows nothing about," as Jesus told his disciples.

It sounds ridiculous to tell anyone that we had rather pray than eat, but is it so foolish? God promises to bless, prosper and provide for those who will "seek Him first."

We tried it and we have found that it is true. In fact, we have found such miraculous answers to prayer, we can hardly wait to get together each day! We can hardly take a day off work...we don't want to miss anything God is doing! Some people will come in at noon, even when they are on leave...just to be with the little group of women who are receiving those promised blessings.

Everybody does have a lunchtime in the Pentagon; but not everybody eats! What happens to people when they give God their lunchtime? It's exciting! God can do a lot in half an hour!

What can happen when you will give God half an hour out of your busy day? Exciting and wonderful things! I hope you will be inspired, to ask a few coworkers to join you, at noon, where you work. Begin to "seek first the kingdom of God," and His blessings will begin to flow through you.

Chapter 9

SEVEN TIMES AROUND JERICO

In the Spring of 1970, a young Marine fighter pilot, who had been active in the men's early Wednesday morning Bible Class, was discouraged over attendance. He had been verbally twisting men's arms to get them into the class and giving them various responsibilities -- but nothing worked. The class seemed to dwindle instead of grow. He decided to fast and pray about the situation, but on the next Wednesday morning, only he and the leader, John Broger showed up!! It was worse instead of better. The two men prayed again for the Pentagon and men working there, especially the leaders.

"Walk around the Pentagon seven times," God spoke to Myrl's heart. It was embarrassing to even think about doing that, so he waited. But he knew God wanted him to walk around the building as an act of faith -- no matter how foolish it seemed. So -- early Saturday morning, Major Myrl Allinder arrived at the Pentagon, alone, in civilian clothes. Hoping no one would see him that knew him.

The first time around he was so discouraged about the lack of men who were concerned with spiritual growth and fellowship; he cried out to God. Silently, of course.

The second time around, he still felt burdened as he prayed and walked. The third time around a few of the guards looked at him quizzically as if to say, "that guy went by here a little while ago." Myrl continued to pray for the people in the Pentagon and an outpouring of the Holy Spirit.

The fourth time around he began to feel good -- faith began to rise in his heart. He was smiling now and numbers of work crews had started up and were outside doing various tasks around the building.

He noticed the people were staring as he went around the fifth time, with a "who is this guy?" look on their face. He felt exhilerated! God could do anything! And he knew God was going to move the hearts of the people and draw them by His Spirit.

The sixth time around, the work crews stopped and looked; the guards leaned out to see if he was coming around again. He was. He was really marching for Jesus. He could tackle the world! "Bring on the devil," he thought, he could handle him. He really felt God's blessing by now.

He wasn't even tired as he made it around the Pentagon the seventh time -- he waved to the guards and workers. By this time their eyes were popping out! "Who is this nut?" He felt high -- he was going to do some great and mighty things in that Pentagon, for Jesus -- yes, sir. He was God's man and ready to go!

Then God spoke and humbled him "suppose I want to use a washer woman in the basement and not you?" He could hardly speak -- it really hurt when he saw his own pride.

Myrl replied, "Could I help carry her pail?"

He headed home to ponder all this in his heart. He was a busy officer, in a busy place, and seemed to always be rushing somewhere and never enough time. But God had heard the prayers and began to move in that big building. Several prayer groups began to meet for breakfast. Navy Commander Carl Wilgus was used by the Lord to spark some new groups. John Broger faithfully met and he too began several new groups of high ranking civilians and officers gathering one morning a week for prayer for the nation and its leaders. Some groups developed into Bible studies. The groups were growing in numbers and enthusiasm for the Lord. John Broger's original group met every day now, 7:30-8:00 a.m., and other groups were springing up.

In 1972, the men invited the ladies from the Bible class to join with them for the morning devotions, led by John Broger. What an answer to prayer! The women had heard of the exciting answers to prayer, testimonies, etc. and had been praying about being included in the group -- the first morning Jean Johnson and I were on the "front row" bright and early.

It was exciting to hear men like Colonel Jerry Curry, Colonel Troy Alcorn, Major Myrl Allinder, Bill Allison, Ernie Bockstance, Colonel Bill Wilson, Bob Brown, Colonel Jim Bennett, Colonel Jim Meredith, Bob Schneider, Roland Heyden, Lt. Cmdr. Jerry Roberts, Colonel John Gonzalez, and Lt. Commander John Elliott share what God was doing by His Spirit. Truly we went to work refreshed and up-lifted by this fellowship of believers.

The little Meditation Room was packed -- people came in at various times, due to schedules of busses and carpools, but came even for a few minutes of refreshing, springing up from the move of the Holy Spirit.

Some came early, about 6:30 a.m., as much as two hours before work -- in order to pray and have ministry for special needs. It was thrilling to see the power of the Holy Spirit work in ordinary people, as blessings of healing, deliverance, salvation and baptism in the Spirit came about.

One incident was astounding -- only three people were present about 6:30 a.m. and a young black soldier came in and flopped in a chair. He was welcomed and asked where he worked -- he stammered a reply. Then everyone began to share prayer requests and he didn't have one, so we went to prayer.

"I feel the Lord wants to heal you, young man," a Marine officer, Major Myrl Allinder, said. The silence was brief and the young Army man began to weep. Through his tears, he related he had suffered horribly from stuttering all his life, and doctors had been unable to help him. He was so ashamed of this disability -- he just wouldn't talk to people.

"Do you believe Jesus can heal you?" "Yes."

"Do you want us to pray for you?" "Yes." And we gathered 'round and laid hands on him and prayed briefly.

"Thank Jesus for what He has done," Major Allinder told the handsome, black soldier. And the soldier began -- "t-t-thank, t-t-thank you." The Marine spoke with authority but quietly, "come out of him, you foul spirit, in Jesus name, loose him and let him go."

The soldier's eyes opened wide and immediately he began to praise the Lord Jesus -- no stuttering, no faltering, no speech problem at all!

He laughed and cried, all at once it seemed. He thanked Jesus and hugged us all as he practically ran from the room to go and tell what God had done for him. By then we were almost in tears, for the mighty miracle we had seen in our midst.

Soon many other early morning "pray-ers" joined us, as the regular 7:30 a.m. time approached, and they too rejoiced over the miraculous healing.

Everyday was a blessing -- you didn't want to take a day off and miss what God was doing in the Pentagon!

The women came to the group in greater numbers, but never forgot it was a men's group and we were invited guests. It was wonderful to see these ladies were content to be supportive and didn't have to be in leadership to feel equally loved and worthy as the men.

However, there were opportunities for women to be aggressive and take over leadership, when the male in authority would occasionally be away. But the sweet and gentle spirit of the ladies prevailed. Thank God for it! These fine Christian men were often quiet and the group could have been dominated by a few outspoken women, and the make up of the group could have soon changed to a women's gathering.

Those of us ladies who had been part of the morning devotions since the original invitation was given in 1972, made it a point to inform new ladies who came, of our privilege to be invited and remind them it was a men's group. Praise God for the unity and love of the Spirit. We felt protected and cared for -- like sisters. The men treated us as older brothers would, always quick to pray for us and counsel when we had a problem arise. We could always call on them when we had a real need and feel that special brotherly love and concern.

Brotherly love was evident one day when Mrs. M. had a serious problem. She was a widow, nearing retirement, a sweet Catholic lady, always jolly, whom everyone loved. The day she called Major Allinder, she wasn't jolly -- she was serious.

"I need prayer at lunchtime," Mrs. M. said. "I've got this pain -- it's so bad I can hardly get my breath."

Major Allinder replied, "I'm due at a meeting at one o'clock. I don't --"

His voice stopped in mid-sentence. "That's my lamb," God said, "care for my lambs, I will take care of you."

37

"I'll meet you in the Meditation Room in five minutes," he answered and immediately called me and several brothers to meet there with him. We prayed for Mimi with no visible results. She was in great pain.

Then the door opened and Rose came into the room. Rose was a small, attractive black lady, who worked in the basement "Goal Post" snackbar. Her hours kept her from attending most of the Christian groups, but she often popped into the Meditation Room, before work and during her lunch break, to pray.

"That's the woman I told you about," God said to Myrl. And he instantly recalled God had said he wanted to use a humble woman for His glory.

"Come and pray with us," Myrl invited. Rose replied, "the praying is done -- it's time to praise."

Myrl felt anger rising inside himself -- "who was she to tell them they'd prayed enough? They had expected God to manifest His love and power, through a healing touch on Mimi's body -- and nothing had happened as yet. He felt they should keep on praying. What did this woman know about it? She had just walked in.

Before anything could be said, Rose began to dance around the room and praise the Lord!! Her face radiant with the joy of the Lord. Rose danced her way over to Mrs. M., took her hands and asked "don't you know that Jesus loves you and you are very precious to Him? You need to thank Him and praise Him. Come."

With the three men and myself watching, speechless, Rose and Mrs. M. held hands and danced a little happy, skipping dance around the room -- just thanking Jesus and praising God. What a sight to cause joy in heaven -- a young black, uniformed waitress -- and a white middle aged lady circling their arms and skipping and praising the Lord together! I wanted to get in on that -- so I joined them.

"I feel wonderful" Mrs. M. exclaimed! The pain is gone! Oh thank you, Jesus! Oh thank you all for praying for me -- bye." And she literally danced out the door. Rose left also, rejoicing as she made her exit.

The men and I were overwhelmed by the proceedings and had to laugh at how God used a "washer woman in the basement" to fulfill His purpose in Mrs. M.'s life. They were glad they could meet to pray and "hold her pail" -- just the way God had said He wanted them to do.

The time!! It was almost one o'clock!

Each of us dashed out of the room, heading to various offices. Myrl looked at his watch -- he was almost afraid to. He gulped -- he was going to be late for the meeting! He ran all the way. He was the only Major and probably the lowest ranking officer attending. He prayed as he ran -- "Lord, help me."

His heart was pounding as he opened the conference room door -- bracing himself for the hostile looks a latecomer would get.

His eyes popped out!

No one was in the room!

He went in and sat down. Was this the right day? The right room? He looked at his notes -- this was it alright.

God spoke to his heart, "you took care of my lamb and I took care of you." His words of grateful thanksgiving came forth. "Praise God. Thank you, Jesus."

"Sorry I'm late" -- This phrase was repeated over and over as the many others arrived. God performed what He had promised the Marine fighter pilot -- who thought he'd be last, but was first instead.

Chapter 10

ADDICTED!

In the Meditation Room at noon, you will find a group of women who meet every day! They may have been shy the first time or two that they came, but they were greeted with friendly smiles and encouraging words, and soon they were part of our Pentagon family. The Holy Spirit has drawn them from every race and religious background into a close-knit group of sharing, caring "sisters."

God has marvelously answered prayers and supplied needs in the group as we have come together to share, and it has been exciting! So exciting that we want to meet every day...we are really hooked!

Hooked on what?   Love.

Who can resist love?   A family kind of love. Missing anyone who is away; concern that comes from sharing problems and needs together. Crying together and praying together; understanding the hurts and encouraging or comforting during a crisis.   What an encouragement it is...to have someone, in that vast building, who cares about you! Someone who prays for you.   It is a wonderful gift from the Lord, to know you can call someone for a quick prayer...and help is soon on the way! We have a "hotline to heaven" when we agree in prayer, praying in Jesus' name.

Anyone coming into the Meditation Room can see the love between the women is real.   The welcome is always one of delight!   To be together is a happy time and a boost to our spirit and gets us through some pressing office deadlines, or family problems.   The delight in being with other women who love the Lord, shows up in glowing smiles.   There is nothing phony about the joy on the faces of this group where everyone is loving and concerned for each other.   It is one place in the Pentagon, where you will find everyone happy!

Despite differences in education, career status, ethnic cultures or church doctrine, there is unity and harmony.   We quickly acknowledge that it is a sovereign work of the Holy Spirit in our midst, creating a loving atmosphere and an eagerness to learn the Bible.

There has never been any advertising or pressure to build members for the group. Our goal has been to have a relaxed Bible study and then encourage everyone to apply the principles and promises to their lives. It has grown through word of mouth invitations, when a friend would invite another to come to a lunchtime Bible study or prayer group. The women have come to take part in some exciting Bible studies. We've tackled subjects the Military District of Washington Chaplains have laughingly said "they wouldn't touch with a ten foot pole"...because the women want answers and solutions, based on God's Word. It isn't meant to be controversial. We don't use any literature or books, just the Bible and a Concordance to make these studies "tailor made" for our particular topic. We simply want to find out what God says on a particular subject, and then let each woman decide for herself, how to apply what we've learned.

Now, 25 years after the first ladies group began to meet there in the Pentagon the group of women won't fit into the little Meditation Room! We have become addicted!

We are addicted.....
- o To the Word of God
- o To the fellowship of the saints, our "sisters" in the Pentagon
- o To the love of other believers

We can understand what Paul means, in 1 Corinthians 16:15, about being "addicted to the ministry of the saints."

Chapter 11

6 a.m. ON THE ESCALATOR

Bill started work at 6 AM, so he dropped me off at the Pentagon, two hours before my scheduled office hours. It gave me lots of time to pray, study for my Bible Class, or write letters to our two sons, serving in the military. We usually arrived early -- before dawn.

Secretary of Defense Harold Brown pulled up usually ahead or just behind us. He was always serious, ignoring "Good morning, Mr. Secretary," or "Good morning, Secretary Brown," or "Have a good day, Sir." His appearance was stern, somber -- with all the heavy responsibility on his shoulders, who wouldn't be?

One morning, I started into the building. I walked up the first few steps and saw Secretary Brown's car arriving. I walked a few feet more and the Lord spoke to me.

"Speak to him and tell him you're praying for him."

I was startled. I never had any urge to speak to him before, although I'd had many opportunities -- passing on escalators, etc. I certainly didn't want to speak to him now -- a guard ahead and behind him. He probably wouldn't speak to me, even if I did, and the guards might grab me "for trying something."

I started up the escalator and the Lord spoke again, "Tell him you're praying for him."

I looked around to see where he was. By then, he was just getting on the escalator -- maybe 10 feet away. I was scared! Suppose he was insulted? Suppose a guard hit me over the head?

I decided to obey God. I turned and looked at him. "Good morning, Secretary Brown," I said. He saw me and looked down. He didn't want to see me -- or talk to me. But then, I stepped off the escalator and he was still one-half way down. A captive audience. "Sir," I smiled, trying not to be nervous. "I just want you to know, that there are many people, here in this building, who are praying for you."

The guards were motionless. Secretary Brown broke into a big smile! First time I'd ever seen him smile.

"Sir, we know what a big job you have and we pray for you every day."

He got off the escalator, still smiling, he stopped and put his arm on my shoulder and replied, "Thank you. Thank you very much."

Then into his office he disappeared -- I felt such a happy glow inside! I had done what God said. It had encouraged a man with heavy decisions and responsibilities affecting our entire nation.

I shared this "happening" with the morning devotional group and they all rejoiced. Bill Allison led us and we prayed with great intensity, renewed by this "nudge" from God Himself.

That night I told my husband, Bill. He was even more delighted that I had been obedient to the Lord. He felt the Secretary of Defense probably heard only complaints and criticisms and really bore his burdens of office with little appreciation. Bill felt this encouraging message, of people praying for him, was more meaningful than we realized.

It was exciting to think this meeting on the escalator had been arranged by God. We knew it was just when Secretary Brown really needed it. Praise the Lord! God could have used an angel or anyone, but I was sure glad He used me!

Chapter 12

GOD CAN USE ANYBODY!

I had been working in the Pentagon since 1953 and attended most of the special religious programs sponsored by the Chaplains on holidays. But I was totally unaware that there was anything else God was doing in that big building.

God began with the Christian men in the Pentagon, gathering them together for Bible study, prayer and the monthly luncheons. Occasionally the men would invite some of the Christian women to attend their ICL luncheons.

The Lord gave Navy Captain Ken Butler, and Army Major Callenburg, a vision for expanding the International Christian Leadership (ICL) Luncheons and in 1957 they met with Nettie Sides and Doris Treakle and planned a ladies ICL Luncheon group. The Ladies group needed a sponsor to qualify for use of the dining facilities, and John Broger took the Ladies ICL group under his wing. He provided guidance and assistance and encouragement as they organized, and until his retirement.

Nettie Sides was elected to be the first Chairman of the ladies group, which held a monthly luncheon. It was a wonderful opportunity to invite coworkers to come and hear a Christian testimony or teaching. The group was informal, with the emphasis on creating friends and having fellowship over lunch.

The symbol of the group was the Praying Hands. The group always stressed the need to pray for the leaders of our Nation. Nettie recalls that "prayer was always a very real part of this group's activities. Many lives have been touched and the effects are and will continue to reach the far corners of the earth."

Some time after the Ladies Luncheon meeting was well established, the Lord moved on the hearts of several of the women in leadership, to begin a women's Bible Study in the Pentagon. The late Alicia Veride, later Davison, took on the responsibilities of leading this new Bible study group and was the first teacher. Alicia Davison was the daughter of Dr. Abram Veride, founder of International Christian Leadership and the National Prayer Breakfast. Their offices were in the old and gracious home in Northwest Washington, D.C., known as Fellowship House.

Alicia served as hostess at Fellowship House to the many guests and gatherings which constantly filled the rooms. Alicia took time from her busy schedule to come to the Pentagon and get the Ladies' Bible study group off to a good start. She returned often, bringing special guests along, to share some blessing with the Pentagon women.

Always uplifting, always encouraging, Alicia was dearly loved. She was deeply missed, after her tragic death, which occured suddenly while traveling in Hong Kong. Many of the Pentagon ICL Bible members attended her memorial service at Fellowship House. There wasn't a dry eye in the group, when her husband praised her, and her children rose up and called her blessed.

Laura Zirkle replaced Alicia and became the faithful and capable teacher of the Pentagon Ladies ICL Study group. She was a fairly new Christian, according to Nettie, and her spirit and enthusiasm was contagious. The group was greatly blessed, as the months went by, to have many dedicated and capable women teach the Word of God. One such woman, who was well loved and remembered was Joan Hamilton. She was an employee of ICL, and worked at Fellowship House, coming in on Mondays to teach the women's Bible Class. The study usually was taken from Navigator materials. In 1967, Joan returned to her home in Canada and the group was without a leader temporarily.

During this time Navy Capt. Beatrice Truitt led the Bible class. Later Mary Weist, Nettie Sides, Dorotha Winkel, Gladys Lane, Pat Lawrence, Mary Jane Frye, Virginia Estes, Louise Bivens, Rosalee Disney, Barbara Preddy and Maidie Stanley led the group for short periods. These women blessed and helped many women, who came to the group during that time.

Some time in 1967, the group asked retired Air Force Lieutenant Colonel Maidie Stanley to be the teacher and leader of the class. Maidie was greatly used by the Lord, to teach the women's class for six years. She was employed in the Pentagon as a civilian after her retirement from active military service.

Maidie also taught the Ladies' Bible class in her church, and had a wonderful knowledge of the Bible. She had been healed of Rheumatoid Arthritis through the prayers and anointing at a healing service in St. Luke's Episcopal Church. She was living proof of God answering prayer. Maidie encouraged the ladies to pray for big things.

"We have a big God who loves us all," Maidie often said. Her love of the Lord and for the Bible inspired many, many women who attended the classes during her leadership.

I became a member of Maidie's class in the Pentagon in 1969. It was just what I needed! The fellowship was great and I was so appreciative of Maidie's knowledge and love for the Bible. I never skipped a Monday class and wished it were more often.

One incident stands out in my mind. It was time to begin study of a new book in the Bible as we were nearing completion of our study of the book of John. Maidie asked us to pray for the Holy Spirit to bring unity in our decision. The next week, when the class began Maidie asked us to write our choice for a book to study, on slips of paper. When they were gathered and read, there were only two choices. Not content with that, Maidie asked us to fast one day that week and pray about our study. She felt that it should be unanimous.

I went home and fasted and prayed and puzzled over the gentle whisper of the Lord to "study John." I objected. In my own human reasoning, it seemed foolish for we had already studied John for over a year! But the prompting came again, to "study John"...this time verse by verse. Not skipping around or using a guide book, but simply read it, discuss it and learn what the Bible said.

The next week, in class, Maidie asked us to vote once more. I voted for John. It was unanimous for the study of John! It would have been decided sooner, if I had been obedient to the Holy Spirit and not leaning to my own logical understanding.

This second study of John lasted a year and proved to be very exciting. The discussions were great! No one seemed to be bound by their church doctrine, but just hungry to discover what the Bible revealed. During our study of John, we took little "side trips" to look up Scriptures as we came to topics that whetted our interest. We studied Scriptures on water baptism, being born again, judgment, casting out demons, raising the dead, healing and doing greater works -- definately not your normal Sunday School material.

We had a mixed group, including Baptists, Catholics, Lutherans, Methodists, Holiness, Pentecostals and other Christian denominations. Only the Holy Spirit could bring about such openness, teachability and unity. And there was unity, because of the love of God that was being spread through the Holy Spirit. No one could resist love, and the Bible studies were relaxed. No one felt threatened, or offended, or afraid to ask questions as we discussed applying what we had learned to our own lives.

Even though Maidie had retired, she continued to come to the Pentagon, three times a week, to lead the Bible classes! What faithfulness! When Maidie announced her plans to sell her home and move to South Carolina, it came as a shock to the women of the Bible class. Maidie's longtime friend and companion, Anita Preston, was taking an early retirement, and they felt a mutual desire to get out of the "rat race" of Washington. No more traffic and high prices! They wanted to find a small town home and settle down. We could understand her desire, but we couldn't imagine how anyone could ever replace our dearly loved Teacher! Again, Maidie was so practical, assuring us that God already knew who He wanted to lead. Maidie told us to pray and seek God's guidance, and if we were in unity, there would be just one name...it would be unanimous. Maidie prayed for the leader to be God's choice.

I prayed and felt a gentle nudge that it was to be me. But again I argued with God that I couldn't possibly teach the class...I didn't have the time that Maidie had to prepare. I prayed over each name on our attendance roster, and only one name seemed to lift my spirit, so I felt surely that it was going to be Lillian Whitmore, and not me. But the very next week, in our class, Lillian announced that she was retiring early, and would be leaving in a few weeks!

Again on my knees I sought God's will for the teacher. By this time I knew it was to be me. I just told God that I was willing, but

I felt so inadequate and without Him helping me there would be "no way" I could ever prepare the lessons or teach. I shared my feelings of inability with my sister, Hazel. How wonderful to have a sister who loved Jesus and loved me so much! We shared everything...we were so close...she was my special gift from the Lord. I wondered if I would have ever been saved, if it weren't for her prayers for me?

"Don't worry," Hazel said, "if God is calling you to this, and I think He is, He will do the work and make it easy for you."

What a weight lifted off my shoulders! I realized I didn't have to do it all. I could relax and rely on Him! He would give me the wisdom and the time to be a good teacher.

The old "me" was still a bit nervous, however. When it was classtime, the following week, I prayed and asked God to "show me positively that I was the one He wanted," by having it unanimous on our first vote. If there was even one vote, for another person, I would know that He had someone else in mind. Just a small miracle, please!

We voted, after prayer, and Maidie read the tiny slips of paper. She smiled and announced that it was unanimous...every vote was for me! I was still overwhelmed, but knowing God's promise, that Hazel and given me, "faithful is He who has called you, who also will do it." I wasn't scared anymore, but I knew who was going to do the teaching. I just wanted to be yielded to His will and not mine.

Maidie then said "she had been given a prophecy from the Lord," that very morning. It was for the ladies of the Bible class, and for me, in particular. She said she wanted to wait to read it, until the voting was finished...to confirm that the Lord had spoken to her, that I was the one He had chosen to lead.

April 14, 1973: "Oh my child, know that I love you with a love that will never fail. I have chosen you to do a work for me. Do not be afraid or concerned, for I am in this work and will lead and guide you in it. You will be used in a way you never dreamed of, for I want to move in that building, in the lives of those ladies -- to teach them my Word and commandments; that they may learn of Me and honor Me and know Me. Lives will be changed and My Word will come alive, not only in you but others there in the Pentagon. Know that My hand is upon you, accept my calling and follow Me in obedience and love. Do not be concerned about your ability. I will speak through you. I will show you what to say and what to do. Just be submissive to My will and stay in My Word. Love and obey Me and it will all come to pass. I love you and want to do a mighty work through you. Be patient and do not run ahead of Me. Let Me lead and learn of Me; that others may know Me and My love. Know that you are mine and I need you and will use you, there in the group. Submit to My leading and let Me work in you. The desires of your heart will be fulfilled. Be not concerned. Just trust me and let me work in you; that which I have planned and that which I want, for each of the ladies. Behold all things are new. I want to make of each of you, something far beyond what you want and yearn for. I want you to be like My Son -- perfect in every respect -- ready for My Kingdom. Have courage and let me work. I am with you and will not leave you. You are mine. Let me work in you."

47

What a comfort! What encouragement! What admonition for me not to run ahead of the Lord, not to be fearful and concerned for my own ability, but to let Him work in our midst, what He wanted to do in the lives of the women there. There was, and is, always, the possibility of me, the leader, running ahead and not letting God work as He wants. My prayer continues to be that this prophecy will be fulfilled, and that I won't get in God's way, but be yielded to His Spirit guiding and teaching us all truth, that I might hold lightly the leadership of this group of ladies.

Seeing them get saved, get baptized in the Holy Spirit, and have their prayers answered! God shares this joy with me. I realize all too well that I can do nothing without him. Absolutely nothing of my own ability or cleverness of speech can accomplish anything for eternity, but through the power of the Spirit and in the name of Jesus and through faith in His blood, we can pull down strongholds! We can all glory in the Lord, not in ourselves.

One day Jo Kenyon came to class and handed me a paper and asked if she could share it later on with the ladies. This is what it said:

3 November 78

Nita, the Lord spoke to me during the night, (not in a dream, I was wide awake) and He showed me your face and gave me this message!

"Because she loves me and has obeyed me, I have granted her request. Those she leads (the class) have been given "the" gifts. She (Nita) is mine and she is yours."

She clarified.

"You are the Lord's, and He chooses to share you with us. You are our gift -- a blessing to us from the Lord. PTL! I have not shared this with anyone -- I was to give this to you, that you might share it."

Love in Christ -- Jo Kenyon

I was very touched, and encouraged that God would do this for me! I called on Jo before the class ended, to read what she had written.

Someone asked me once how I knew I was a teacher. Well, God has always given me something to teach each week, and He has always given me someone to teach, who is teachable. It has been easy. God has really made teaching easy. I recall God's promise from 1 Thessalonians 5:24, that "He also will do it," if He has called you.

That was May 20, 1973. How honored I've been to be part of this Bible class! How good it has been to see God bless our women and the studies we've had! Nine years is a long time, but it has flown quickly past. Now thoughts and plans for my own retirement are taking shape.

Who will God choose to take my place? The little Meditation room is crowded now, where will this little "Gideon's band" meet? It's so wonderful to be confident that God already knows! It's so wonderful to know that God can use anybody, even me!

Chapter 13

MAIDIE - THE WALL FALLS DOWN

Our study of the book of John, verse by verse, proved to be a turning point in Maidie's life, and life changing for many other women who knew her.

The book of John contains so many references to the Holy Ghost, it was puzzling to most of the ladies, who had never heard of the Holy Ghost!! Some had sung the Doxology, "Praise Father, Son and Holy Ghost," but knew nothing more. Maybe they didn't want to hear about a ghost! Maidie explained the Holy Ghost and the Holy Spirit were one and the same.

It certainly made Maidie desirous to know about the Comforter Jesus promised to send, when He ascended to the Father. So we studied. Maidie dug into every aspect and we learned much about the Holy Spirit, who He was, His work to glorify Jesus and teach us and we studied about the fruit of the Spirit. We learned a lot!

When she said we were finished, my heart really sank. How could we be finished without a study of the gifts of the Spirit, or the baptism in the Holy Spirit? After the class, I talked with Maidie privately about these topics. We agreed to meet for lunch and discuss them further.

My! Did I pray! I had felt I was the only person in the Pentagon, who had been baptized in the Holy Spirit! Little did I know! I really longed for someone to talk with, about this second blessing from God. I had prayed for a spiritual friend with whom I could share my heart, and truly feel as close to, as my sister Hazel, who had moved from the area. I missed her so.

God was about to answer my prayer!

At lunch the next day, Maidie expressed a deep interest in the gifts of the Spirit and we read I Corinthians 12 and 14 together. We both agreed we wanted to see them working in our churches today. We certainly needed the gifts of healing and miracles and to discern spirits of good and evil.

The other gifts were puzzling and we talked about them. I shared my own limited knowledge and experiences. I felt like a mountain climber -- reaching down to help someone just below, to come a little higher, then stretching up to get a hand from someone so I could climb higher too. Faith in Jesus and the Bible was the strong rope linking Maidie and I.

The lunch time flew past and we both wanted to meet again. I went away rejoicing that Maidie was so open to subjects her church neglected. She must have read those chapters all night! At noon, the following day, she was full of questions.

Dear Maidie! How I loved her and loved her thirst for more of God! God loved it, too. He poured out His blessings!

I had told her of my experience of seeking and receiving the Baptism in the Holy Spirit. An unknown prayer language was the evidence, just as recorded in the book of Acts. Maidie was really interested and asked some searching questions. She seemed relieved to know that mine was a quiet experience with the Lord -- at 5 a.m., alone in my kitchen -- no dramatic emotional event.

She had heard some bad reports of tongues, being from the devil, that it was really blasphemy and cursing God! And it was definitely not for believers, after the first century. However, we had read the scriptures that said it was a "blessing" and "giving thanks well" and "glorifying God." Not one time did it say blasphemy.

It truly was amazing that Maidie could be open at all, to receive my testimony and not shy away from me as a fanatic. It had to be the Lord's work, possibly a result of two years of friendship in the Bible Class, and observing for herself that I didn't seem too wierd. Maybe I was a bit excited and exuberant about the Bible being true, and everything available for us today, but I wouldn't add anything to the scriptures, just enjoy them!

Our third lunchtime together, to discuss the Holy Spirit, was a real climax!

"Surely you don't believe everyone should speak in tongues, do you?" Maidie asked.

"No," I told her truthfully, "only those who believe." I added, "that's what Jesus said in Mark 16:17-18." Maidie describes herself as speechless at that point, and she was. I urged her to get alone with God and ask Him for everything He had for her.

Then I told her she could pray for 20 years and never speak in an unlearned prayer language -- unless -- she was willing to be a "fool for God." The child-like faith that comes from believing God's word is essential -- Luke 11:13 says, "God will give the Holy Spirit to those who ask" -- and I told her to ask. Then it was up to her, to begin to speak the little syllables, the Holy Spirit would put in her mind.

"No one expects to talk in an unknown tongue," I explained, "somehow they think the Holy Spirit will do the talking -- like a divine radio! They think that nothing is required of them."

I urged Maidie to step out in faith, and speak the words, as the Spirit gave them even though they'd sound foolish. Naturally they would seem silly, since she wouldn't understand them. But a miracle would take place -- not that she would talk, but that she could talk supernaturally, in a language unknown to her. I reminded Maidie that Romans 8:26-27 tells us that through the Holy Spirit she could pray the perfect prayer to God, for every person, including herself, and every situation.

Jesus is faithful. He is the baptizer with the Holy Spirit and He said, "Ask and it shall be given unto you; seek and ye shall find." He never lets you down. He didn't let Maidie down either.

She called me the next day, and told me that she had received her prayer language, alone, in her bedroom. Just asking and receiving. I was so thrilled and excited! But Maidie was cautious.

"I don't think I really need to tell anyone about this, do you?" she asked me.

"No, if you don't want to, you surely don't have to." I replied, "but one of these days, God will stir up the fire He has kindled in your heart and you won't be able to keep quiet about what He has done."

Then I reminded her that we must be like Paul and make a determination, daily, to pray with our spirit, as well as with our understanding, and to sing with our spirit. Otherwise we would seldom use our "new tongue" and simply rely on our understanding.

Maidie asked me to speak to the class the coming Monday and tell my testimony and answer questions that might arise. I was happy to have a chance to share, but wondered how it might be received. Maidie and I agreed to fast and pray.

Class time arrived and Maidie opened with a prayer and called on me to relate my experience of receiving the baptism, by Jesus, with the Holy Spirit. I did. At the conclusion, you could have heard a pin drop. Total silence! There didn't seem to be any reaction. No one was happy, no one seemed upset. I was a little disappointed, that no one wanted to know more about the baptism or how they could receive it.

Maidie was pleased that it had been accepted so well, by some members, whose church doctrines were opposed to this experience as valid for today. Later in the day, however, Maidie was to hear from a number of women, all afraid she might "stir up a hornet's nest" with anything so controversial being discussed in our class.

Always one to pursue peace and harmony, Maidie felt we had covered enough about the Holy Spirit -- at least for the present. She felt that God would bless the testimony I had shared, and create a hunger in many hearts; for more of God and the power of the Holy Spirit.

The class resumed the study of John. It took another year to complete, but we learned so much. We were thoroughly blessed as we did our verse by verse study.

After receiving her own beautiful prayer language, Maidie hungered for more understanding of the gifts of the Holy Spirit and their operation in the church and ministry of the believer. We spent lots of lunch hours studying scriptures in her car. It was more satisfying than any food we could have eaten. I suggested some local charismatic prayer groups and meetings where she could hear wonderful testimonies or Bible teaching on topics related to the supernatural work of the Holy Spirit, such as, New Adventures in Prayer, led by Jack Zirkle, or House of Bread, led by Bob Grant, The Bible teaching was outstanding and the praise and worship so uplifting, people never wanted to go home.

All these opportunities for teaching and testimonies helped answer questions for Maidie. We had such delight at lunchtime, sharing new things she saw and heard and learned each week.

"Maidie, how would you like to come to a home prayer meeting with us?" I asked.

"I would really love to see what it is like," was her response.

The following Wednesday night found us driving down to Davidsonville, Maryland, to the home of Navy Lieutenant Commander Bob Wright. The house was already full of people. They hugged and warmly greeted Maidie, even before I had a chance to introduce her!

I took her into the kitchen, to meet our hostess, Mary Jane Wright, who was finishing up some punch to serve after the meeting. It was a lovely, big kitchen and reflected Mary Jane's charm and gracious hospitality. Everywhere you looked there was something to remind you that Jesus had first place in their lives. Over the table hung a large, beautiful painting of Jesus and the children gathered around Him. This caught Maidie's eye and she admired it, as I had done before. We remarked over the yummy cakes that were on the table. It was a special night. Bob and Mary Jane were celebrating their wedding anniversary. Mary Jane said, "We'd much rather spend the evening with people who love Jesus, than anything else we could do."

Several of the couples, who had helped start this little prayer meeting had brought cakes, too. you could always count on Myrtle and Nellie Parlett to think of some way to show their love! About that moment, Ron Ciccarone and his wife, Judy, arrived and she, too, brought a cake, which was verbally appreciated by the group of handsome young Midshipmen, who were doing their greeting near the food table!

Reverend George Taylor and his wife, Patsy, arrived and I was so delighted to see them and could hardly wait to introduce Maidie! George pastored a church for many years, and this new life in the Spirit was the result of a need in Patsy's life. Her dear friend was dying of cancer and it made Patsy upset to think the days of miracles and great healings were removed with the early Apostles! All the church offered now was prayers for comfort. It caused them both to earnestly seek God for more power in their lives and in their church. They had been blessed with an outpouring of the Holy Spirit in a life changing way.

George and Patsy took a real interest in Maidie, especially when I explained this was her first visit to a home prayer group. "Maidie teaches our Ladies' Bible Class in the Pentagon, and she's just a wonderful teacher -- we really love her," I told them. But I didn't tell them she had been baptized in the Holy Spirit...she still hadn't shared that with anyone except Anita, her friend and roommate, and me.

From the living room a joyful song had begun and everyone scrambled for a chair, except the young people, who had already taken seats on the floor around the piano. It was crowded. Everyone sang with gusto and six or eight tambourines joined with the hand clapping

52

to "make a joyful noise unto the Lord." The songs were taken from the scriptures and I kept busy locating them, so Maidie could follow along and join in.

Some of the people began to dance as they worshipped the Lord. I glanced to see Maidie's reaction to this form of praise, which was new to her. She loved it and was swaying to the music! So was I. It was all we could do. It was too crowded to move very much between the rows of folding chairs.

A hush fell on the group -- a total change from the praise that preceded it. It was a quiet expectancy -- no one moved -- you could feel the presence of the Lord. A prophecy came forth, "to encourage the people to continue to praise and worship the Lord; that it was pleasing for His people to come before Him with praise and He was in our midst." A harmony of voices blended together as people began to worship God, in the Spirit -- singing in their unknown language and also with their understanding. It sounded like a heavenly choir of angels must surely sound -- perfect harmony, yet unplanned or unrehearsed.

During this singing in the Spirit, I had a vision. I was awake, but it was like a dream. I saw a high wall and it was long and stretched in the distance a good way. Then the wind began to blow -- leaves fluttered on nearby trees. The wind blew harder and the wall began to move -- just one end of it at first. Then the whole wall swayed and fell down! It collapsed rather slowly, but it all fell down! Yet the wind didn't disturb the trees; just a gentle rustle in the leaves. The huge wall was gone. So was my vision.

I wondered what it could mean. I immediately prayed and asked the Lord for the interpretation. The revelation came quickly -- the wall was the church doctrine and teaching that had been a hinderance to the moving of the Holy Spirit in Maidie's life. It was gone! She was free, from this night forward, to receive the power and work of the Holy Spirit. Praise the Lord!

I looked over at Maidie. Her hands were raised and she was worshipping the Lord, singing a lovely song, in her prayer language -- just blending in with all the other melodies. I knew she'd never be the same again -- after this night of freedom. She'd seen and experienced the freedom to praise and worship the Lord, as the Spirit led. I knew she'd never be content with less -- God had spoiled her and let her "taste the new wine" of the Spirit. The old would never satisfy her again. I understood that for it had happened to me, too.

After the meeting, I shared my vision with George Taylor and he quickly agreed that Maidie would never be the same again or content in her present church. He recognized the desire for more of the Holy Spirit, fellowship, and teaching.

It was a glorious evening. Maidie asked questions all the way home -- she was so thrilled over everything. She had a real touch from the Lord -- just about the time I had my vision. She didn't have to struggle to learn the words to the scripture songs -- the words came easily, as the songs came forth. The Holy Spirit helped her learn words and melody, so she could join in relaxed worship and praise. She knew it was a supernatural blessing.

One thing that really astonished Maidie during that home prayer meeting, was the silence that took place -- as if someone commanded it -- the joyful songs stopped and every sound ceased. She had never experienced anything like the calm, yet the anticipation of God's blessing.

"It had to be the work of the Holy Spirit for 50, or more people to get quiet at the same time! And without anyone instructing, or insisting, on it," I explained. "But God wanted to speak to us words of comfort and encouragement and He had to get our attention." And He surely did!

It all fit together, just like our heavenly Father had planned! What a wonderful evening God had worked out, just for Maidie. That night the wall fell down and set her spirit free!

Chapter 14

TOO EXCITING ?

Under Maidie's enthusiastic leadership, the Thursday prayer group became pretty exciting. Often in the past there had been general prayers, nothing too specific in some of the requests, but gradually faith began to rise as God answered prayers for individual needs. We had several women healed, while we prayed for them, and even though "laying on of hands" was new to a lot of the ladies in the class, they read it in the Bible and could see it worked. God honored His word! It was so exciting we could hardly wait for Thursdays to arrive, and see what God would do.

Maybe it got a little "too exciting" for some women, whose churches taught that miracles and healing weren't for today, except through medical skills. We agreed that God does heal that way, but He was also doing some supernatural miraculous healing, often right there in that tiny little Meditation Room in the Pentagon.

Still some of the women were upset. The result was splitting up into two groups. Maidie was emotionally torn over the division. It wasn't over a big church doctrinal problem. It was over the issue of healing! Some felt the Pentagon was no place to pray for healing. Others did.

Maidie was asked to omit any further prayers for healing, or study of any controversial topics. She resigned from her position as teacher of the ICL group feeling she couldn't continue with such limitations. A number of the women didn't want to continue in a group with such restrictions. There were no harsh words, just a silent pulling away from others. The ICL luncheons continued each month. It was as though nothing had happened on the surface, but the fellowship had been broken. Everyone seemed to be happy, except God.

The Chaplains office granted use of the Meditation Room two more days a week to be used by the women, and a small "charismatic" group was formed, meeting Wednesday and Friday. God blessed both groups.

In December of 1971, Maidie began teaching the charismatic Bible Class and it was wonderful to have the freedom to study topics that might be controversial. People were saved, baptized in the Holy

Spirit and miraculously healed. Some of the ladies asked if we could meet in a Conference Room on Mondays too, as they missed having the fellowship and study on that day. Maidie came three days a week. We felt God's anointing on our studies. In May of 1973, when Maidie turned the leadership over to me, we continued to meet three days a week.

Our Charismatic class began a study of healing scriptures, and it was exciting to have each woman bring in verses they had found, and we discussed how they applied to us. It was like a gigantic love letter from our heavenly Father. We knew everything He wanted for anyone in the Bible, He also wanted for us today. Women were healed, as their faith grew. It was exciting to see what God did for women, as we met to study and pray. It was evident that God was blessing us. So we "must" be in His will, wouldn't you agree?

On a Monday morning in 1977, about 5 a.m., I was praying, prior to dressing for work. God spoke so clearly to me. "How can you say 'I have no need of thee? Can the eye say to the foot, I have no need of thee? Is it not part of my body?'"

By my withdrawal from the ICL Monday Bible Class, I knew exactly what He meant. I was saying that I didn't have any need for those women. They didn't believe exactly as I did. They weren't an "eye," so I didn't need them! I said all this by my actions, not by any words. I argued with God. I know it sounds foolish but I've done it! He has never been harsh, in response to my questioning or justifying my position. Kindly and gently He has made His point.

"But God," I told Him, "look how you are blessing our Monday group! People are getting saved and baptized in the Holy Spirit, and healed." I continued, "You know that would never have happened in the ICL class."

God spoke softly, but firmly, "I want you to be one."

I still didn't see what was coming next, so I replied, "Well, Father, you could have those women come to my class. I'd be glad to have them. I'll even start going to the luncheons again."

"I want you to support their class," God said, "I want unity." How could such a gentle voice, be so firm and final?

On the way to work that morning, I told Bill what the Lord had said to me. Fully expecting him to agree with me "that surely God wouldn't want me to give up my class." That this must be a test, just to see if I was "willing" to do His will, just to see if I was "willing" to give up my Monday class and join the other group.

"Well, if God said it," Bill replied, "you'd better do it." That wasn't what I wanted to hear!

So I reasoned with my husband, who had always been so supportive and helpful to me and to the class. I reminded him of all God had done in our class and how it wouldn't have taken place in "the other class." Surely God wouldn't want to set aside such a wonderful ministry!

Bill's logic was so simple. He was thinking far ahead of me. "If God wants you to disband, no one will come to your class today! Then you can contact them during the week and tell them you won't be meeting again on Mondays."

"Okay," I told him. "Perhaps you're right. If that happens, then I will know God doesn't want me to continue, even one more week." Down inside, however, I felt pretty confident that this would never happen. The women were much too faithful. One or two might not come, but for no one to attend? It just wouldn't happen!

During the morning, I had to pray a lot about the situation. I had to examine and reexamine my yieldedness to do the Lord's will. I asked myself if I was holding too tightly to a Bible class that was His, and not mine? Over and over again I assured the Lord I would accept His will, and would join the other class "if no one showed up" during the noon hour. I admitted I didn't want to, but I would, if He wanted me to. He did.

I couldn't believe it! Not one person entered that Conference Room during the entire class period! God had made it abundantly clear! There was no getting around it. This was our last meeting. I cried. I still found it hard to believe, God would disband the one I taught, where His word was believed so fully. His ways were certainly not my ways!

I called each of the women who had missed the class. Each had a special problem, or reason, why they hadn't been able to be there. None of the women wanted to dissolve the class. I could only tell them what God had said, and urge them to support the Monday class. I told them God wanted unity, and if I was at work, I would be in that ICL class from that day forward.

It wasn't easy.

That first Monday, when I entered the Meditation Room, the ladies in the class hardly greeted me. They must have felt I was there to spy! They were shocked and bewildered by my presence, I'm sure. I had never met the woman who was teaching the class at that time. She was just a delightful person with a marvelous sense of humor and I couldn't help but feel at ease with her.

I had thought that somehow they would know God had sent me. Or they would ask and I could tell them of disbanding of my own class for the sake of unity. No one asked. No one said much one way or the other, and I could see I made them uncomfortable. I went back every week. I enjoyed the class and felt sad there were so few attending. The teacher always had a knack for sparking our thinking on the Scriptures we studied. I prayed over the empty chairs. That little room had been full when Maidie taught it. I could see why God wanted unity. The division had hurt everyone, even though we'd covered it up pretty well on the surface.

I began attending the monthly luncheons and enjoyed them so much, I realized I had only hurt myself by staying away. No one had even missed me! About a year later I received a call asking if I would serve as an officer for the ICL luncheons. I really didn't want to. I had enough to do already. I was teaching the Wednesday and Friday classes and helping get a new class started on Thursdays. But I agreed I would take a small position, after they insisted they wanted me to serve. After the phone call, I thought I had it made. I told the Lord I would serve if every vote was for me. If even one was for anyone else, I would feel free to say "no." With so many non-charismatic members in the ICL, I felt confident it wouldn't be unanimous.

It was unanimous. I had been elected for Chairman, not the small office I'd said I might consider. What could I do? I had told God I'd take it, if it were unanimous, and I did.

The women told me they felt God wanted me to be the Chairman, as He wanted unity amongst the women. I still had never told any of them about what God had done to bring us back together. But God had also worked in their hearts the desire for unity. I had wonderful women to plan and serve with, and it was a joy. Elections came and went, and for three years I was unanimously selected for Chairman. Each time my prayer was the same, if I were to serve, it had to be clear cut, unanimous. No one had ever served that long. I was sure they'd want a change, but they didn't seem to. They really honored me and made me feel special.

But God wasn't through with me yet.

Arranging a program for the year, my first term as Chairman, I wanted to invite a speaker from Fellowship House who had helped in the ICL Monday Bible Class. I knew she'd be a fine speaker and would bless the women. As time for the luncheon drew near the Lord began to work in my heart. It was so humbling I cried even thinking about it, but I knew the nudging was from the Holy Spirit. I wanted to do His will and it wasn't easy. My pride stood in the way.

"I'm particularly happy to have a guest speaker here today from Fellowship House, as well as some of our retired ladies and others who are out of the building now," I told the large group of smiling women over lunch. "I want to ask you to turn in your Bibles, if you have them, to I Corinthians 12."

I read what God had said to me almost two years before about one member of the body acting as though it didn't need another part of the body. When I finished reading I said, "I want to ask your forgiveness. I am guilty of saying that I didn't need some of you."

My eyes were full of tears. My heart was broken. What a terrible thing to confess to all those women! But God had showed me that my spirit needed to be broken, that I needed to ask for their forgiveness.

"I ask you to forgive me, for breaking away and for hurting you. For thinking that I was more spiritual than you were." That's about as far as I got. I wasn't able to control the tears.

Our speaker got up and hugged me, several of the women did. There was a healing that took place that day. God poured heavenly balm in old wounds. God brought about the unity amongst the women...at last. The Pentagon people know us Christians by our love for one another.

In 1981 the leadership of the Monday ICL class opened. Soon it was announced that Marlene Zerbe, the daughter of Alicia Davison, would be leading. Alicia had led the Pentagon group when it began, so this was delightful news. Marlene was just as beautiful as her Mother. She brought along Ronda Royalty, who would assist in the teaching when Marlene was out of town. Ronda graduated from Oral Roberts University and works at Fellowship House. Both women are full of the joy of the Lord, faith and the Holy Spirit.

58

Chapter 15

SEVEN HEADS ARE BETTER THAN ONE

"I can't make all these decisions by myself," I told Bill, as we drove home from work.

"Now that Maidie is gone, I need someone to help me decide about details for our annual retreat and selecting someone to keep up our name and phone number listing, since Lesley is gone." It was good to be able to share all my problems with Bill! God had given me such a wonderful husband, I never get tired of praising him!

"You should ask several of the ladies, who have been faithful attendees over the years, to serve with you and form a board of directors. That way you'd have a good group to make all the decisions and they could help with tasks that make the class better," was Bill's advice. His management and leadership skills provided the insight I needed.

"June Whited is taking care of our lending library and Annette Harrop is handling our tapes," I went on. "I'd want them to serve, of course."

"And Jean Johnson," Bill added, "has been the most faithful woman in all the classes."

"You're right," I agreed, "she's the person who invited me to the Bible class the very day I had prayed God would lead me to a group!" I reminisced about Jean and how we'd met. God has a sense of humor! We'd met in a ladies rest room early one morning in 1969 and I remarked how refreshing it was to hear someone singing a hymn so early in the morning -- in the Pentagon! That led to a brief conversation about our mutual faith and Jean told me about a small Ladies' Bible Class meeting once a week in a conference room. We agreed it was too bad it wasn't advertised -- for I'd been in the building almost 16 years and never heard of it! I couldn't wait to attend! I was so delighted over the Lord answering my prayer, I couldn't keep quiet! I told Jean what happened, "I prayed at 5 a.m. this morning for God to lead me to a Bible study, where people really believed the Bible -- and here it is 7:30 a.m. and He's already answered!"

Jean smiled and said, "Isn't the Lord good?"

I found Jean was loved by everyone -- so modest, so faithful, and always willing to help.

"Oh, honey," I snapped out of my happy daydreaming, "I want to ask Gertrude Davis to serve, too! She has been so faithful and helpful. She'd be a good treasurer, if we had any money, because she's good at collecting for gifts and things."

"That's five, counting yourself. That ought to be enough," Bill said, "but seven is a perfect number!"

"Kathy White has so much faith. I'm going to ask her, too," I decided. Dicey Beverage was our seventh member. God rewards faithfulness and so did we in selecting women. Everyone agreed to serve on a "Council Ring" when I asked them. We wanted it to be very informal, to meet only when we needed to plan retreats, special celebrations, or make decisions on matters affecting the class.

The Council Ring hasn't changed much over the years. We've had our annual retreat expand to four a year and have decided to extend an invitation to husbands, whenever we have a guest speaker that would appeal to them. We have been blessed by this group of seven counsellors. Decisions for class activities and our ability to serve the class have been easy with capable and willing women. Vicki Egan, Nancy Beauschesne, Lesley Redfearn, Debbie Jansen, and Peggy Martinez have also served in leadership positions on our Council Ring.

Jean Johnson serves as Vice Chairman of the current Council Ring. Susie Ezzell has been treasurer since Gertrude's retirement. Cindy Mulroney does a little bit of everything as our Secretary and helps everyone, especially in coordinating our retreats. Pauline Hayes is in charge of our large tape lending library. Tapes from all our monthly ICL luncheons, guest speakers at retreats, testimonies and Bible teaching are available. Tilly Fowler is our librarian. She brings a variety of Christian books to class each week. She is such a joyful person, "I can't help smiling and saying praise the Lord," Tilly says, "for Jesus changed my life." Everyone brightens up when Tilly comes in the room! Our newest member is Genny Grinkley, who has been shy and quiet all her life. Now she tells everyone how Jesus has given her confidence and freedom from fear through knowledge of the Bible. Genny keeps our name and address list up to date.

I have to pause right here and tell about a dream Genny shared with us. She saw Jesus in the midst of our class! We were happy and circled around Jesus waiting expectantly. Jesus was smiling and He began to feed us some bread. We were so hungry! We all eagerly ate the bread and He gave us more and more. She awoke and was so happy and encouraged, and couldn't wait to tell us the dream.

What a dream!

How wonderful that God revealed we were coming to Jesus as children, not proud and wise adults. We were sure He was going to provide for us, as we waited eagerly. He gave us bread! Thank God, we weren't satisfied with a little bit, but were hungry for more. It was easy to discern the bread was His Word for Jesus said, "I am the bread of life." May we always hunger and thirst for more of Jesus!

I mustn't forget mentioning three ladies who were exceptions to our seven members serving on the Council Ring; Janet Evans, Marie Yates and Loretta Howard. They were "guest advisors" who were asked to come and serve on numerous planning sessions. We just loved and appreciated them so much, but felt we should stick to the number seven as permanent members of the Council Ring.

Janet Evans had endeared herself to every one over the years. She was capable and efficient in any task she undertook and helped as a liaison, along with Al Munn, between the various men's and women's Christian groups. Jan served on many Pentagon Prayer Breakfast Committees and her faithfulness was a blessing to all.

When I was asked to start a Thursday Bible class for women in 1978, I said I really couldn't take on anything more. However, I agreed to get it started and we'd pray for a leader. The four young women who asked to start a class were just new Christians and wanted to cover some basic Bible topics. They needed help with their questions. Was it worth hours of study and planning for just four women? You bet! These were little lambs who could easily go astray and needed spiritual food to grow on. Someone had led them in a prayer, using the Four Spiritual laws booklet and here they were -- one step in the kingdom and wanting to know more.

I met with them three or four weeks and a few more ladies came, too. I loved it, but I realized I couldn't and shouldn't do everything. As I prayed about someone to teach this class, Jan Evans kept coming to mind. I had asked God to guide me and if Jan were His choice, she wouldn't hesitate but readily accept. Since she had not taught before, I knew this would be asking a lot, but I also knew that God gives us the desire and ability to teach. I was living proof!

"Thank you for asking me, Nita. I would really like an opportunity to teach, and "Bible Basics" sounds like something I could handle," was Jan's response!

We discussed it and agreed Campus Crusade for Christ or Navigator study guides would be helpful teaching aids. Jan taught the class, which grew in numbers and spiritually, for two years before she retired. I loved being in the class, too, and thanked the Lord for her willingness to teach. God is so good!

Marie Yates was our "hostess with the mostest." Petite and bubbling with the joy of the Lord, she and her husband, Bud, opened up their lovely home for many of our retreats. We were always so welcomed and they assured us "it was the Lord's house." Anytime Christians wanted to get together and praise the Lord, they were quickly invited to the Yates' home. Bud even spoiled us a few times by making his famous cream puffs. So Marie was included as an "honorary member" in our planning sessions for retreats.

Loretta Howard was recommended by the Council Ring to teach a women's Bible class for a group of ladies who couldn't attend at noon because of later lunch assignments. Maidie had taught a class at 1 o'clock, as well as the 12 o'clock class on Wednesdays. Since she was retired, she could stay as long as she felt necessary. After Maidie's departure, that left a big void in leadership. Several women had expressed a desire for a later class.

61

There was no one who wanted to assume this position for several years, until Loretta got promoted to a new position. Her new lunch period was later and she offered to take on leadership of a class, one day a week. This was an answer to prayer! Loretta was an older woman, knowledgeable of the Bible, and of godly character for setting an example by actions as well as words for the women in her class. Loretta's class has studied faith and produced some women of prayer. She has served as a guest advisor on several occasions and she has sung for several of our luncheons. Loretta has a unique position of helping visitors to the Pentagon, who stop for information at the concourse desk. Her helpful, friendly smile and manner put the bewildered strangers at ease.

God has made leadership easy, by giving us a multitude of counsellors! Dear sisters to help lead, and willingly serve in whatever way is needed to support prayer and Bible study in the Pentagon. Indeed! Seven "heads" are better than one!

Chapter 16

ONLY IN THE BUILDING

"Please pray for me, as I'm going on a job interview," Kathy said. "I really need the promotion and it is the only job that has come open here in the building." Kathy White was a pretty, auburn-haired woman, who commuted from Fredricksburg, Virginia, daily.

"My husband just doesn't understand why I won't look for a job outside the Pentagon. I told him "I'd have to hear God speak in my ear, if I ever left. The Christian fellowship means too much to me."

Kathy was highly qualified and very capable, but the competition was stiff for management positions. We knew God could raise up, or put down whomever He chose. We knew He "rules in the affairs of men" as the Bible declares.

We prayed for His will to be done. Kathy got the promotion and stayed for three years. But God needed Kathy in other places, to share her faith and get more women praying, so He helped us to say goodbye when she left the Pentagon.

"I'd wash dishes just to work in the Pentagon, and be part of the women's Bible studies," Nancy Beauschesne, shyly told the class. "I've turned down several job opportunities outside the building. The money just isn't that important to me."

Nancy was single, in her twenties, with a lot going for her, besides her modest good looks. She was a Smithsonian tour guide on weekends, President of the Pentagon Toastmistress organization, ballroom dancing competition enthusiast and, most of all, keenly interested in Bible study. Nancy was like a sponge, she just soaked up the Bible studies and started applying God's principles to her own life. Naturally there was a change in her life! We would study a topic and Nancy would always go and discuss it with her Priest. She'd been raised with Catholic schooling and was very faithful. The Priest would always encourage her to keep growing spiritually and was happy over her studies of the Bible. She measured everything by God's plumbline -- His Word. It was a joy to see the Bible come alive in her.

"I'll never leave the Pentagon," Nancy said. "This is like having a family, right here in the building, with all my sisters to love and care for me." But when God's time came, Nancy did accept a promotion out of the Pentagon. She found a noon-time Bible study at her new job, and quickly joined. Then she began studying with several friends from her apartment building during the week, and also joined a Navigators group. Nancy has kept close to her Pentagon family, attending our quarterly Retreats. Some of the "family" attended her water baptism at Barcroft Bible Church. God is blessing this pretty young woman, who was born again, in the Pentagon Ladies' Bible Class. She didn't want to leave, but God had other plans!

We miss everyone who leaves...just "like family." God has moved women away from the Pentagon family, often to distant places around the world. They have gotten busy to start Bible study and prayer groups in their new homes. It's thrilling and exciting to see God multiply His family and His blessings, in this way, as little groups of women gather to pray and to study His Word.

No one wanted to leave...with one exception!

Chapter 17

ONE EXCEPTION

One young lady, who worked as a secretary, wasn't content to stay in the Pentagon. God took her from the "Pillars of the Pentagon" to the jungles of Papua New Guinea! During her junior year at college, Karen Adams saw an opportunity for an "easy" course that summer which would provide ten credits. She took it, even though she wasn't interested in the subject of Linguistics. That course changed her life! God used her natural desire for ten easy credits, to get her into His service. The course was taught by a Ph.D., who had been involved with translating Bible portions. It challenged her! It inspired her! At last, she knew what she'd like to do with her life. She signed up for the required Jungle Camp training, which was held in the desert wilderness of Mexico. If she had a weak prayer life before...this was certainly the cure for that!

The requirement to spend eight weeks alone in the jungle, in small groups of two to four, armed only with bare necessities, was enough to make anyone think twice about becoming a Wycliffe Bible Translator! In "advanced" jungle training, you lived in a mud hut, with no floor, electricity or water, but it was shelter!

What a way to spend your summer! When Karen successfully completed that, she was ready to go wherever Wycliffe would send her. Her parents were concerned about their only daughter going off to some remote jungle. Karen asked the Ladies group to pray for God's will in her decision and a year later, Karen was leaving for Paupa New Guinea, with her folks blessing and prayers! The Pentagon women promised to pray continually and many to support her financially.

Her prayer-letters were full of interesting details of her work in the jungle base camp. There, the translator teams from many villages would come to finalize translations, rest and work on Primers and other materials to take back to the villagers. One of their tasks was to teach the people to read and write their own particular language. It seemed strange, to us in the Pentagon, that there were whole tribes of people who had never seen their language written down!

Karen worked at the base camp print shop and we prayed, with her, for a girl who would want to be her partner. Linda Lauck, who was also working at the base camp teamed up with Karen and they were selected for a tribe.

They were sent out with another translator for their first weekend in a village. They didn't know a word of the language! But the people were friendly and they were treated as sisters by the men of the tribe. As Karen and Linda sat with the women and children, observing them work and play, they began to learn words and make up an alphabet. Karen and Linda liked it in the village and tackled the assignment of Bible translation with youthful enthusiasm.

The villagers were helpful, as well as curious. Karen wrote us that they liked to touch her hair, which was long and blonde, comparing it to their own course black hair. No matter what they did there was always an audience. Especially when they had a tiny house built in the village. It contained a flush toilet. Karen wrote that everyone had to come and flush it and laugh over this new contraption. The girls also had a big tank built for collecting rainwater, so they didn't depend on the river for all their water. This proved to be a blessing to the villagers in dry seasons. Karen wrote and asked for prayer during the construction and especially that God wouldn't let their water tank run out. This was a testimony of God's provision to the villagers, that God did supply all their needs. They never ran out of water. This must have impressed the villagers, many of them had been tempted to join the Cargo Cult, which Karen wrote us about. This Cult lured people to join by promising that their god would supply the "cargo," or needs, of it's members. We agreed, as we wrote to Karen, that truly we did have a God who supplied all our needed "cargo" for us!

Karen and Linda are still in Papua New Guinea. They have completed more than half of the New Testament, plus some of the Old Testament. We're still praying and supporting their efforts. We're very proud of the one girl who didn't want to work "only in the Pentagon."

Chapter 18

PLEASE BE PATIENT

"Practical training for daily living would be a good title for our Wednesday Bible Class," Neyna Darcy told the ladies a few days before she retired. "These Bible studies have been so helpful in learning how to overcome problems at home, or in the office I'm really going to miss this group." We knew we would really miss Neyna too, her faith and friendship combined into a sweet, sweet spirit, not easily replaced!

"It has helped us recognize that our difficulty in getting along with others, is often our wrong attitudes," Jan Farr said. "We think we are so important that everyone should treat us special, and when they don't, we get angry! Jan concluded, "We like to think we're sweet and don't get angry, or have feelings of bitterness, but we are still very human, and we do."

"We know that Christian women shouldn't act that way," Marie Williams chimed in. "Instead of always feeling guilty or unworthy because of our failures, we've learned to repent, then get up and try again to reach the goal of becoming like Jesus."

"It's wonderful to know that God doesn't give up on us when we goof," Amelia Richardson added.

"If there is any sweetness in us, it has to be the Lord!" Jean Conours said. "But we're learning that we have to pray and ask God to help us change. We can't do it alone!"

"You know, I thought when you became a Christian, you changed immediately to a new person," Eloise Rice responded. "But our Bible studies have helped me see that we have to do what God says. We have to "put off" our temper tantrums. We must make a decision to change! We somehow expect God to do it, and yet His Word says, 'you do it'."

"That's right, Eloise, God says to "stop lying; stop gossiping; stop complaining; stop stealing, etc. ...it sure doesn't sound like God is going to do it for us," Gertrude Davis said.

"That's not all," Gerry Beard remarked, "these Bible studies have taught me that we have to "put on" gentleness and patience. We do that by deciding not to react the way we used to. We decide to have a forgiving attitude. We decide to love an unkind person. We decide to only say good things about people or to them. Once we decide, then God will help us do it."

Lillian Whitmore chuckled, "Thank goodness, God isn't finished with us yet. We're still growing and changing."

"It helped me when I realized that the Bible is full of 'commands' and not 'suggestions'," Jean Johnson told the class, "Corrie ten Boom had a real sweet way of saying that, when she was here to speak at the Pentagon."

"Perhaps one of the greatest accomplishments of this Bible study group has been to help us be better employees," June Whited said. It was true. Our studies often related to us as working women, and what our attitudes and conduct should be in difficult situations. God had a way of testing our obedience, by giving us situations that were sometimes unfair.

"When I first started attending the class, I asked, 'Who should fill the water jugs for the coffee? Shouldn't the Officers and I take turns?'," Peggy Martinez wrote in her Christmas letter. She was enjoying being home with her three children now. It was an answer to her prayers. But she missed the caring and sharing fellowship of the Pentagon women.

"You always taught right out of the Bible, and it impressed me that what you said, Nita, wasn't just your idea or opinions." Peggy continued, "I was beginning to feel 'walked on'. The first thing I would see when I arrived in the morning was the water jugs on my desk! Just waiting for me to fill them. I felt hot anger rise up inside me for that. Your answer to me, Nita, was 'Do it for Jesus.'"

"After that, every time I filled the water jug, I did it for Jesus! Now I loved filling those jugs, and I couldn't wait to do it! It changed my whole attitude about the office. Love presided where anger was what I felt before. It was a miracle, and very important. I received five Outstanding Performance Awards in my ten years at that job!"

I had told the women in the class, that we should make a difference in our offices. We should try to do the best work, without mistakes, without grumbling. We should set a good example by not being habitually late nor asking to leave early. We shouldn't argue, but submit to the authority God had placed over us. The Bible says...'Not only to the gentle but to the stubborn, rude and offensive.'

"You always encouraged us," Martha Allison said, "reminding us that we shall receive a reward for every good thing we do!" God has rewarded the vast majority of the women in the Bible study classes, and they have received superior performance ratings and awards often supplying a financial need.

Such was the recent case with Jerri McClanahan. "Our Bible studies have helped me have a better attitude about my job. This year, I received an outstanding award, with a Quality Salary Increase," Jerry told us, "I really needed the money and this was an answer to our prayers."

"I can't always get out of my office at noon to get to the Bible studies," Carolyn Robertsen said, "but I know I need to be cheerful and willing to cooperate in my job. Who in the world would want to be a Christian, if all they saw was a grumpy, complaining one? I get so much out of our studies and fellowship, though, I really hate to miss it."

"It helps us military girls, too," Specialist Shirley Dryden added, "to realize that God has placed our bosses over us, and if we rebel against them, we're raging against God's authority! Jesus died for them, and we are here to pray for people, and love them, not hate them."

"The Barracks are my home," Sgt. Carolyn Munford said, "and when I get uptight, I just don't talk to anybody. I shut myself up in my room and won't talk. That's not a good attitude either. I'm glad I have Christian sisters to remind me 'not to lose my joy'. If God never answered another prayer, I should still be a joyful person after all He has done for me."

"I remember the teachings about making the Pentagon a better place to work because we are here," Terri Borden told us, "about picking up paper towels in the Ladies room, and keeping things neat and clean. Being willing to have a servant's heart...it helped me a lot."

We were very thankful for the military women who attended our Bible classes. We knew it wasn't easy for them to live for Jesus. Life in the Barracks was not like home. Barbara Minniefield was always bringing someone new to class, someone who needed a friend, someone who was discouraged, or disillusioned and needed prayer. God answered prayers for many of these pretty young women, who were active in their Base Chapel Programs; Faye Hargrove, Sandy Brown, Tina Woods, Cathy McDaniel, Linda Mims, Paula Bryant, and others who have come and gone over the years. We knew they were a great blessing and could reach a lot of other young people in the Military Services who needed a ray of hope when they were discouraged.

"The beautiful teaching about being a 'sweetheart' to my husband, and not a nagging wife, really helped me," Jessie Bailey said. "I realized that I was taking my husband for granted. I needed to change and I did. Then my husband accepted the Lord and God really has blessed both of us."

"The study on submission to our husband, by willingly allowing him to make decisions and be the head of the home, and just appreciating and enjoying our husbands, was a big help to me, too," Tilly Fowler said. "I'm still learning." We all were!

"These studies will help the single women like Nancy Harvey, Sylvia Sutton, Ellen Hoffman, Betty Boone, Angela Ryan, Kathy Oden and Sharon Jackson, too," I told the class. "You'll be a better wife and maybe you won't make the mistakes some of us did, who didn't know what the Bible said to wives." We think 'our women' are prepared for successful marriage relationships as a result of our Bible studies on home, marriage and love.

"Don't forget your teaching on returning stolen goods," Loretta Phillips reminded us. We talked about what God had done for us to change our attitudes as a result of studying the Bible. It was easy to use a pen, paper clips and dozens of other items which were so common around our offices and then to find we had 'conveniently' brought them home. It was easy to rationalize that they weren't new anyway, or "everyone else did it" or "we'd worked so hard we had paid for these things."

Reading the Scripture that said to "return stolen goods" was hard to ignore! Another Scripture said there would be a "curse in the house of the thief!" None of us wanted that hanging over us! Lots of items were returned to offices and a new resolve "not to help yourself." God called it stealing!

"He didn't say it applied only to "big" things either!," Gladys Woodard said.

These and many other topics were studied in our Bible classes. It was practical training for daily living. It accomplished what God wanted it to do. It changed many lives.

Chapter 19

"A" IN RELIGION

"I got an "A" in religion in high school, but I don't feel like I know anything!" Cindy Mulroney told me after her second visit to our Bible class.

"You know a lot more than I did when I became a Christian," I told her. "I didn't come from a Christian home and I never heard anything good said about Churches or the Bible. So I didn't know the books of the Bible nor where to find them. I figure if I could start learning at 40 years old, anybody can learn!"

We were on a study of the Baptism of the Holy Spirit. Cindy was interested because a couple of friends were involved in a Catholic charismatic group and they had been telling her about this change in their life. She had many questions, so she soaked up our Bible study like a sponge. She even recorded our class, so her husband could hear about it too.

"The natural man cannot receive the things of God; they are foolishness to him," we read from I Corinthians 2:14. Then we discussed how many people go to Church faithfully, but get upset when others talk about the blood of Jesus or being born again, or that Jesus is the only way to eternal life.

"Unless you are born again, it seems like nonsense and of course you would argue against the Bible! You just cannot understand spiritual truth without the Holy Spirit," I explained to the class.

"How do you get the Holy Spirit?" Cindy asked.

"That's a good question. Let's see what the Bible says," and I led the class to Luke 11:13. "God wants you to have the Holy Spirit, but you have to want it, and ask for it."

"Let's look at Acts 2:38 and see that there are requirements to receiving the Holy Spirit. First, you must repent -- turn away from your old life, of doing your own thing. Then, be water baptized. Now it won't do any good to get baptized in water, if you haven't done what Romans 10:9-10 says. It's a requirement. Let's read that right now," I told the class. "Keep your finger at Acts 2:38, though."

I called on Phuong Newhart to read it -- I knew she would never volunteer! Phuong was quiet and shy, perhaps because she felt she couldn't speak English very well, but she did, beautifully. Everyone loved Phuong and she was opening up more all the time, responding to the love and hope she received from the ladies. We had often prayed for her family, many of whom she did not hear from for months. They were "boat people," who had escaped from Viet Nam. She didn't know if they were alive or dead or where they might be! A few, she knew, were still in Saigon. But God knew where each one was! And God answered our prayers, and granted Phuong's desire that all her family would come to America. We rejoiced when each one arrived, joyfully welcomed by Phuong and her husband, Bob, who sponsored them. It was a miracle!

Phuong read the verses from Romans 10, using the Bible her husband, Bob, had given her. Bob was a real sweetheart. We all loved the way he'd escort her to the class, give her a kiss and go on his way. At the conclusion he would return to escort her back to her office! "Have you each done what these verses say?" I asked. "It is vital that we meet God's requirements. If we do, then we can be sure we are saved." I probed a little bit. "Have you been really faithful to your church? Keeping all their rituals and regulations? Giving your money and time? Never missing a Sunday? Maybe even teaching a class?" Most of the hands went up.

"Did you know that you can die and go to hell, tonight, if you haven't met God's requirements?" My question had their attention. "Your name must be written in the Lamb's Book of Life, as the Bible says. Who is the Lamb?" I asked.

"Jesus," a chorus of voices answered.

"That's what John 1:29 says, and to get our name there we must not trust in our own righteousness by doing good things, or living a decent life. If we trust in our own goodness, we have not submitted to the righteousness of God, which only comes through faith in Jesus Christ. (Romans 10:3). Good people, who do this, seem "religious," but will be rejected by God! It is a terrible deception satan uses in many large Churches, where salvation and the whole Bible are not taught."

"Would you like to pray a simple prayer, right now; before we go into our study on the baptism in the Holy Spirit?" I asked. "Just to be sure of your salvation?" A number of heads nodded "yes," so we prayed, and all repeated after me:

"Heavenly Father, I thank you for the Bible. I thank you that every word is true. I want to obey your word. Right now, I repent of my sins. I ask You to forgive me and to come into my life. Help me to be the person You want me to be. Heavenly Father, Your word says 'Jesus died for my sins.' Your word says 'He died and arose on the third day.' Your word says 'He ascended into heaven.' Your word says 'He is seated at Your right hand, and He is coming back again.' I believe it. Your word says 'if I believe in my heart and confess Jesus is Lord with my mouth, that I will be saved.' I believe it. I am confessing it now, before others. I thank you for your promise of salvation, and I thank you, right now, for saving me. Amen."

"Now we are ready to receive the Holy Spirit baptism, just as the people did in the book of Acts," I told the class. "Let's look up Scriptures and see what happened to them." We looked up the incidents in Acts, where the men of Ephesus had become believers, but hadn't received the Holy Spirit. Peter and John were sent to them, prayed for them to receive and they did. No one had to wonder if they received the Holy Spirit for the outward sign was the same as on the day of Pentecost. They all spoke with tongues. Then we read about Cornelius and his friends and family, who received the Holy Spirit, even though Peter didn't pray for them. It was a sovereign work of the Holy Spirit, to pour out this gift on the Gentiles. Until then, the disciples wouldn't have dreamed the Gentiles could have been accepted the same as the Jews. Then he remembered the prophet Joel, who had said that God would, one day, pour out His Spirit on all flesh! That would include Gentiles, as well as Jews.

"Now, let's turn to Acts 2:39," I said, "and see that this promise of the Holy Spirit is for you, and for your children, and all who the Lord shall call. Anyone who becomes a believer in Jesus Christ has been called, so we see that the gift of the Holy Ghost, or Holy Spirit, is for everyone. But, you have to ask. Remember what we read in Luke 11:13?" I reminded them. "You have to ask, and then believe that God will not give you anything, but a good gift. If you ask for the Holy Spirit, you do not have to be afraid of receiving anything unholy or bad."

"Let's look at Luke 11:9, and see that it is Jesus who promises that everyone who asks, receives. You don't have to try to receive the Holy Spirit. Jesus says that if you ask for the baptism in the Holy Spirit, and the outward sign that those early believers received, that is precisely what you will receive," I continued. "You have a part to play in the miracle that occurs. Just as Peter had to exercise his faith, when he walked on water. Peter knew Jesus could give him the authority and ability to walk on the water, but it required faith to act on Jesus' word, "come." Peter had to get out of the boat and depend on Jesus to do the miracle of making the water hard under him. Peter acted and Jesus performed the miracle, as a result of Peter's faith. And so it was with the miracle of turning water into wine. The people did not need water, they needed more wine. But the servants trusted Jesus and obeyed His words, they acted and filled the jars with water. Then Jesus did the miracle, as a result of their acting in faith. And so it is with receiving the baptism in the Holy Spirit," I told them, "you must begin speaking by faith, and the miracle promised by Jesus will occur. Belief plus action results in a miracle."

"In a few minutes we are going to pray, and you will ask Jesus to baptize you in the Holy Spirit. He will do it, and then at that point, you will have to be very careful. You will speak little syllables and words that are unknown to you. They will sound foolish, any unknown language you hear sounds foolish to you. But you must exercise your faith and speak them out, trusting the Holy Spirit to give you the perfect prayer. Trusting Jesus to give you the good gift He promised to send from the Father. He didn't say to "wait for it, if you were going to be a Missionary or go to Bible School, or be a Minister." No, Jesus said all the Disciples were to wait for the Comforter, the Holy Spirit, to be given. Jesus wants you to receive the power to be His witness, as recorded in Acts 1:8."

"After you begin to speak these new words the Holy Spirit will give you, thoughts will enter your mind. "Oh, that was just me." Or "I don't think that was the gift of tongues, that was just me." Be very careful. It is very serious to blaspheme the Holy Spirit! It is a type of blasphemy to attribute the true manifestation of the Holy Spirit to the devil or to your flesh."

"Now, let's pray for the baptism of the Holy Spirit," I said, and we did.

After class Cindy came to me and softly said, "I really got a lot out of the class today. You know there are so many things I've never heard before. I feel like I've got so much to learn. I wonder how I could have maintained an "A" in religion class!"

"I'm sure you were an excellent student and learned everything you were supposed to learn." I replied. "But God wants us to know all the Bible, not just certain parts. The only way you'll ever learn it is to start reading it every day and don't skip around. Read every verse and every page. It takes time and discipline, but the rewards are like finding hidden treasure. You've got to dig for them!"

Cindy gave me a hug and a smiling reply, "I can't wait to talk this over with Mike. I prayed that prayer today and I know he needs to pray it, too. He's so smart, he'll be able to understand much better than I do and I want us to study the Bible together."

"Wait up, Cindy!" Susie Ezzell motioned our way. "I want to invite you and Mike to come with Gary and I to "Take and Give" next week. I think you'd like it," and out they went with Susie explaining TAG was a big weekly meeting down town, in Washington, that about 2,000 young people attended every Tuesday night. I started praying immediately. I knew Cindy and Mike would be really blessed by the songs of praise and great Bible teaching. Especially since the two young men who led the meeting, Larry Tomczak and C.J. Mahoney, were Catholics too. I prayed they'd go -- just once -- they'd be enjoying some of God's best teachers.

God answered that prayer and soon I was hearing weekly reports on what happened at TAG. Mike was saved and then baptized in the Holy Spirit. He and Cindy received almost at the same time. A year or so later they started a small Bible study group in their home. They're still learning! It's great to see what God can do with someone, like Cindy, who is not satisfied with an "A" in religion!

Chapter 20

BEFORE 8 O'CLOCK IN THE MORNING

"I don't have time to stay this morning, but I want you to pray for me tomorrow morning. I want to receive this baptism in the Holy Spirit you've told me about." The words came, with a beautiful smile, from Mildred Hollberg, as she stood to leave the morning devotions.

"It's something the Lord wants me to have, and I want it, too," she said, "I just feel a bit cheated, when I think that I've never been taught this in my church, all these years. But it's not too late, is it?"

"It's not too late." "See you tomorrow." "We'll be praying for you."

Mildred was planning to retire from her job soon. We would miss her beautiful faith and cheerful attitude -- she was an inspiration! The rest of us just hoped we'd have her enthusiasm and vitality when we reached 70! Her husband was dead and her only son and his family lived in Richmond, so her plans were to move there when she retired, and enjoy her grandsons!

The next morning she was early and so were others. We were expecting a real blessing and God never lets you down! The leader, Bill Allison, read the scriptures to reinforce her knowledge of this "promise of the father" that Jesus said would be sent to His followers, after His resurrection. Acts 2:38-39 assured her that it was for her, and as many as our Lord Jesus called. Praise the Lord! Then we gathered 'round and laid hands on her and began to pray. Almost immediately Mildred began to weep. The more we prayed, the more she cried. Through her tears she told us, she "had something to tell us -- tomorrow -- when she could talk and not cry."

I went around to her office, at noon, to see how she was doing. She was beaming and couldn't wait to tell the ladies' class what had happened that morning. I wanted to hear it, too! All I could say for sure was "she had a good cry."

"I was so afraid, when they prayed for me," Mildred told us, "I knew they were expecting me to begin speaking, in a language unknown to me -- and I didn't want to disappoint them." "But I speak Swedish and Norwegian and German also. I was so afraid I would just begin to worship the Lord, in one of those languages, and they would think I had received my prayer language. But I would know I didn't," she continued. "So I didn't want to say a word, or let out a peep, that wasn't unknown to me." "All I did was cry," she said. "But God didn't let me down -- the Holy Spirit gave me words to say, words I didn't know, but I'm afraid no one heard them, for all my tears."

"Do you suppose it's OK, if I ask God for an interpretation? I'd really like to know what I'm saying." We told her, "That's where faith comes in, you won't know what you're saying." But the Bible says "you are talking to God" and being edified yourself, as you speak in the new language given you by the Holy Spirit. You just trust Him to give you the right words, to pray the perfect prayer everytime," as Romans 8:26-27 said. "It would be all right to ask God to give you an interpretation, once in a while. The interpretation edifies the church, just like prophecy, and it would encourage you. However, you don't want to have any unbelief, as the gifts operate by faith, not by our own understanding." That answered Mildred's question and she beamed that beautiful smile. "I'll do it! I want to pray a perfect prayer, for my family, every day."

God can do a lot before 8 o'clock in the morning!

On the day of her retirement, Mildred wore a beautiful dress, in the colors of her beloved Swedish flag. It was a happy, yet sad, day to say goodbye to a precious sister in the Lord.

She entered the Hermitage in Richmond, Virginia, and began a ladies' Bible study and prayer group with the residents there. God used her love for His Word and her love for others to draw the women to the group.

Chapter 21

100 MILES TO PRAY

"Our program director would like to invite the ladies from the Pentagon prayer group to come and hold a prayer program here," Mildred wrote us. "There are so many who need strength and encouragement -- and bring your harps, too. They will enjoy the scripture songs." The class agreed it would be a wonderful opportunity for Jesus to bless them and us! So we accepted the invitation to drive 100 miles to pray!

Eight women arranged to drive down for our first of many prayer programs to be held there, by invitation. We were so delighted that Maidie, our former Bible class teacher, and her friend Anita, were up for a visit from South Carolina, and could join us there. Everyone was praying for God's love to be poured out -- and it was!

We expected perhaps 20 to 30 people and about 200 came! We felt so overwhelmed and insignificant in that large, stained glassed chapel. We really knew God had to take charge since we weren't capable of anything, except sharing what God had done for us and praying for His blessing on them. And that's what we did!

Each lady shared a brief testimony of a miraculous healing or answer to prayer after we had sung a couple of songs. It was great to ask them to open the Bibles in the pew racks, and follow along with us. We sang Psalms, as David did, and played on our harps! Then I spoke on some "reasons for unanswered prayer" and assured each person they were very precious and important to God. Then, based on Romans 10:9-10, relating God's requirements for abundant and eternal life, I invited everyone to join in a prayer of repentance and to permit Jesus to take charge of their lives as Lord and Saviour.

After our program, we invited anyone who needed a touch from God to come up for prayer. It was a blessing to see these dear little women slowly coming down the isle, some with canes, some helping others to walk. Their needs were great. We were glad they were coming to Jesus for help, for we couldn't do anything. But He could and He did.

One little woman had asked for prayer and as we prayed, God released her crippled hand. She was so excited! "I can see my thumb!" she cried out, "I can see my thumb!" And there it was, restored to normal. We praised the Lord for the miracle we witnessed, and knew He would be glorified as everyone knew of her previous condition.

Another lady had a hearing problem, even with a hearing aid. After prayer, she was able to hear without the device. She cried and so did we. We knew we couldn't make her well, but Jesus is the same today and He never turned any one away who came to Him for healing. Our confidence was in Him! Several more people with hearing aids came and all were able to hear! Even a whisper! PTL!

It was so exciting no one wanted to leave. After we prayed for each of them, we asked these ladies to stay, and pray with us for others. Afterwards, a resident who was a former missionary thanked us, for including that prayer and opportunity to receive Jesus and salvation through faith in Him. She felt this invitation was often neglected. We returned once or twice a year for more prayer services and each time God blessed our going out to visit these lovely people. Each time we were so blessed by their welcome and appreciation.

One trip is still very vivid in my mind. Maidie and I were asked to go to the Infirmary prior to our program to pray for a woman who was scheduled for surgery. She couldn't attend, but asked us to come and pray for her. She had been unable to walk for some time due to a crippling disease which left one leg shorter than the other one. The doctor was going to graft in a bone. It sounded horrible. She was in a sun room sitting in a wheelchair when we arrived. She was all smiles and expecting us. We knelt down to look at her leg. She pulled back her robe and my heart sank. It was at least four inches shorter than the other leg! I had seen God lengthen and straighten arms and legs and backs before -- but nothing like this!

My first thought was, "It's impossible." Then my faith rose up. It wasn't impossible for God! He could do anything and it didn't depend on me at all, except to pray a prayer of faith. I could do that all right, for I had seen God do miracles. I knew He wanted to show us His love and power.

There were three or four nurses sitting nearby and, standing in our midst, was the one who had wheeled this sweet lady into the sun room for our visit. I didn't know what they would think about a couple of fanatics praying for a miracle, but we didn't have any choice. It was almost time for our meeting to begin! So Mildred, Maidie, and I prayed and laid hands on her. I asked Mildred to hold each foot in the palm of her hand and just watch what God would do. This was no time for closing your eyes, we would "watch and pray."

We hardly began praying when the short leg began to move down. We thanked the Lord for hearing our prayers and watched, rejoicing as the leg continued to stretch slowly downward. It was breathtaking! We got pretty excited with our "Thank you, Jesus" and "Praise God." The nurses were all looking at us. The dear little lady in the wheelchair was crying and so were we! How great is our God!! Her legs were evenly matched -- a miracle occured right before our eyes. I asked her to get up and walk but she wanted to wait and get a "walker" to help her. We heard afterwards she walked and amazed the doctors and staff. She didn't need any surgery for God had done it! PTL!

God did a lot every time a handful of women were willing to drive 100 miles to pray.

Chapter 22

OIL AND MEN

One meeting at the Hermitage was unique. Although it was announced as a "ladies prayer meeting," there were four men present! Mildred Hollberg, our hostess and sponsor, sensed my concern, as I try never to be in a position of teaching men or having authority over them.

"These are retired Ministers who are residents here at the home, they would like to be here as observers," she told me. Then I could understand their position and probable concern. As reports from our previous meetings reached them, it may have sounded like some pretty "unusual" things going on. They may have felt the need to come and check us out. Whatever the reason, here they were. So I welcomed them and acknowledged their leadership there. I restated my obedience and desire to teach only women, but as observers they were most welcome.

After our testimonies and singing, I shared "Principles of answered prayer" from the Bible, then it was time for acting on the Word. I asked those with needs to come forward, and said that we would lay hands on them and pray a prayer of faith. God was going to bless each one who would act on this invitation.

"Ask the ministers to come up and do the praying -- and anoint the sick with oil," it was a word the Lord put in my mind.

We had never anointed with oil and didn't advise our women to do so, as we felt that ministry was for the church elders. We women could lay hands on the sick and pray in Jesus' name, which we always did. As a "coincidence," that particular trip, we had several ladies join us who were new to our class, and one brought a bottle of oil! She had offered it to me earlier but I explained we women didn't do anointing, just praying. So -- here God had provided the oil and the elders to do the ministry! That was exciting. But would they do it?

I invited the ministers to come up and pray with us, for those who were sick. I explained we would like them to anoint the sick with oil. For a few moments, not one of those four men moved. Maybe they were stunned! This was new to them I was sure.

"Gentlemen, won't you please come and take the authority God has given you, as ministers and elders, to anoint and pray for these dear ladies?" I asked. "We came to pray for then, and we will; but we don't anoint with oil." We don't fully understand why God wants the sick to be anointed with oil, but He says to do it." I concluded, "God honors our acts of obedience."

One man stood up and glanced around at the crowd and headed down the isle! As he did, another followed. And then another. The last man sat with his wife near the back. She helped him down the aisle -- he needed healing himself! We discovered, as we asked their names, that this minister also had great difficulty hearing, even though he wore a hearing aid. We had to repeat things loudly for his understanding.

These precious men of God asked what they should do? None had ever anointed the sick, but they were willing. Praise God! We were just thrilled and knew God had a blessing in store for them -- and us!

The women came up for prayer -- a long line. The first woman had a "unique" experience, the minister poured oil right onto the top of her head; in the middle of her freshly done hairdo! Then he, and the other men, laid hands on her. Then he prayed -- it was a brief rather halting prayer -- but she rose up radiantly exclaiming she "felt better already."

We had asked the men to take turns, doing the anointing and praying. We Pentagon ladies joined hands around them and agreed in prayer. As the men prayed, their faith increased. Their prayers became louder and longer and full of faith in God's promises.

The women from the Hermitage loved it -- being prayed for by their own men. God loved it. He answered mightily that very day, healing several people instantly. The Pentagon ladies loved it -- having those ministers so willing and so excited about being used by God in a new way.

We suggested they might offer to be available in the future to pray for any sick who might want to be anointed with oil, and have laying on of hands. We rejoiced during the 100 miles back to the Pentagon. What a meeting. It was so nifty knowing it was God's program. We couldn't heal anybody of even a headache, but our part was being willing to go and pray. Then we could relax. It was God's promise to us. "Lay hands on sick, pray in Jesus name, and they shall get well." It was up to Him to do it. We could relax, because the healing wasn't up to us. Our God is so creative! There is always something fresh and wonderful happening, if we just make ourselves available. He'll do the rest! Our blessing that day was 100 miles away from home! It was worth the drive!

Chapter 23

THE WEDDING

One of the happiest times for our Pentagon ladies was showing God's love as a "family" to our dear sister June. She was so precious to the women in the class. She had a child-like faith in God that was inspiring. She was well educated, efficient, capable and certainly not childish in any way, but took God's Word literally as His promises for us today. If God said it, that settled it for June!

Whatever topic we studied in class, she wanted her pastor's opinion on it. Her pastor had to think about things he hadn't confronted since Seminary. June asked him about such things as annointing with oil and laying hands on the sick, water baptism and examining yourself before communion and taking it unworthily. June wanted to know her church's position on these things and she totally respected and appreciated her pastor's views. She knew he respected her too, but did feel as though he took a side door sometimes to avoid meeting her after some of their discussions!

The class had prayed for June's son, Brian, as he advanced through college and went into the Navy. We were so proud of his achievements and prayed over each exam and rejoiced over excellent grades. Many of us felt so close to him, through shared news written to his Mom, and our frequent prayers for Brian. We all agreed he was so thoughtful and considerate toward his Mother and we loved that fine quality, especially since most of us were mothers too, and we desired the same characteristics in our sons!

It was almost graduation when the wedding date was set, while Brian and Susan were home for Christmas holidays. What an exciting time! We had rejoiced over their engagement and a mutual desire to please God in everything they did.

We knew June's family was scattered long distances away and her own Mother's recent death left her facing a happy, but lonely occasion. What could a few women do to show our love and support? To reinforce her position of being very special and loved by the "family" she had in our Pentagon Bible Class? We decided we'd like to prepare a festive rehersal dinner to honor June and show our love for the wedding couple. We didn't know if they'd even accept the offer! Maybe they wouldn't want a home cooked "homey" dinner. Maybe June would want to go all out and have the dinner at the very best restaurant. But we offered.

Too late. She had made plans for the finest steak house. She was pleased and overwhelmed by the thoughtfulness and said she'd bring it up to Brian and Susan.

"Why would they want to do all that for us?" was Brian's response. "Just to show you and everyone present how much they love us," replied June.

"What do you think?" June asked.

"How could we refuse such kindness?" Brian answered.

It was set, and plans began for a meal they would never forget. The food had to be elegant and the tables had to be lovely. Ladies brought their best china, silver and tablecloths. Everything was coordinated perfectly. Only God could arrange for so much matching of table pieces.

My Mother, Delma Jenkins, graciously volunteered to cook and be in charge of the dinner. A sigh of relief came from Kathy White, Jean Johnson, Jan Farr, Annette Harrop, Edith Wickert and me, the women who had undertaken the project! Mother had owned several restaurants in Anchorage, Alaska, and had been well known for her fine cooking, especially her pies. She made over 90 each day and said they were sold out by noon. So, the menu for the wedding family had to include "Delma's pies." It did, coconut cream and chocolate.

The day of the dinner arrived. The ladies were excited over what lay ahead and prayed everything would be perfect and show forth the love we felt for June. Several women took the whole day off, others half a day. We met at the big lovely church and spent hours setting tables and decorating the room. That is, everyone but Mother. She was busy on pies and baking the huge ham.

We took a little break for lunch and found Mother almost in tears! The stove wasn't working properly. It was electric. It had two settings operating, high or off! We couldn't believe it! Mother had prepared filling for eight pies and burned it, after finding the stove wouldn't work on any setting but high. We made a fast trip to the store to replace all those dozens of eggs, sugar and milk.

We all prayed. More ladies arrived to help and joined in prayer. It looked like we might not have a dinner at all. Only God could help.

After prayer we contacted the church office and were assured the stove worked "fine" as no one ever reported any problems with it. We knew we had a spiritual battle on our hands, an adversary, who would like to spoil our gesture of love and make it a ridiculous affair that would make June, Brian and Susan ashamed. So, we prayed as we worked and sang songs of praise.

Mother started on a new batch of pie filling and everyone offered to help. It was a battle -- all day long. The vegetables were prepared and we discovered now only one burner would work at all! Plus the oven, which blasted away on high. Due to the extremely high heat, the pie crust shrunk out of shape and was unusable. At this rate we'd have to buy more supplies and start mixing pie crusts! "Help Lord! In the name of Jesus!" Cries of distress from everyone's lips.

A new plan was devised. It took longer, but it might work. Pie dough was placed over the outside of a pie pan and another pie pan was laid over that -- so the dough was enclosed and held in shape. We prayed this would work and it did. It wasn't as brown as she liked it, but Mom agreed it looked fine, and did get done without burning. The pie filling took two hours to cook! It required taking the pan off and on the burner to prevent scorching. Everyone felt exhausted. Several more ladies arrived; Jean Johnson, Annette Harrop, Jan Farr. They'd come right from work ready to help serve. They were put to work watching the pies. Mom was finishing putting them together. The meringue was piled high and looked beautiful. Instead of 15 minutes cooking time -- it might only take two or three minutes on that high heat. They had to be watched constantly.

At last! Ten pies were set to cool -- they looked like a page out of "Southern Living." It had taken nearly eight hours to complete them! It was unbelievable! Mom announced she'd "never make another pie." We all laughed. She loved to cook and we knew she wouldn't keep that "declaration of independence" for long.

We were ready for the wedding party and families to arrive. We changed into our matching serving outfits. We wanted to look like professional and competent waitresses, even if we were sweltering in our long black skirts and white blouses! All of us kitchen crew had eaten a quick meal and sampled everything. Praise God, it was wonderful! No one would ever know what we went through, praying over that contrary stove all day!

The soon-to-be bride and groom arrived, June and all the guests. We managed to control our joyful emotions as we greeted them and ushered them into the banquet tables. It was so beautiful, all candlelight and lacey white wedding bells and flowers. June's friend, who was not from our Pentagon Bible Class, Edith Wickert, had spent the morning arranging flower bouquets and ribbons on each table, another love gift for our beloved June.

June popped in the kitchen to say "hi" to the crew. She was beautiful and radiant. Her pearl grey dress was very elegant and yet simple. It really highlighted her golden hair. We were so proud of her! What a beautiful mother. We knew Brian was feeling proud of her too. After being properly hugged, June enthusiastically relayed the remarks on the beautifully set tables and the decorations. She thanked everyone for their love and hard work.

"Time to serve, before this food gets cold," Mother said, and June hurried out to join the others.

The blessing was said by Brian, thanking God for the love they were shown by friends. The dinner was festive, lots of good conversation and laughter along with the beautiful food. People may have been full, but no one declined when pies were served, and they tasted as great as they looked. The kitchen crew had to sample, just to be sure of it, naturally.

All the ladies were asked by Brian to come into the banquet room after the meal. We didn't really want to -- but he wanted all of us there for the final prayer. He introduced us as June's friends from the Pentagon Ladies' Bible Class and everyone applauded! Brian prayed a beautiful prayer from a heart overflowing with love and thanksgiving to God, and it perfectly finished a lovely evening, giving a foretaste of the happy wedding events to come the next day. June lavished us with glowing praise. Her joy was worth every minute.

As soon as the church cleared, the ladies collapsed into chairs, exhausted. Too frazzled to even clean up. We prayed claiming the promises in Isaiah 40:31 and new strength came. To our amazement we felt great and we danced around and praised the Lord. Then we swung into action clearing dishes, only to arrive in the kitchen to find Jean Johnson washing the pots and pans. She insisted on washing everything. She was the sweetest, prettiest and best dressed dishwasher you ever saw. We all agreed there was no one like Jean to willingly tackle the worst job with joy.

We kicked off our high heels and sang songs of praise as we worked. Time flew past. We had such great fellowship as we cleaned! It was a joy to do it when it was for the Lord's kids. It was almost midnight as we left the church, still excited and not really feeling tired. The joy of the Lord was our strength.

The next day June looked radiant in pink from head to toe as she danced with Brian at the lovely wedding reception. He was dashing in his white Naval officer's dress uniform. How proud she was of him! And we were, too. We felt like family.

A beautiful bride and handsome groom. That is what fairy tales are made of -- but this was no make believe story. Brian addressed the happy congregation after the minister concluded the wedding ceremony. He vowed, as did Joshua, "as for me and my house we will serve the Lord." Who could ask for more?

Their commitment to each other that day was "topped off" by a commitment to the Lord Jesus.

Chapter 24

THE CHAPLAIN CARES

Sometimes God used the Military District of Washington Chaplain to share his abundance with ladies in the group who had an emergency.

One such crisis was a young woman, with two small children, who had been deserted by her husband. As a secretary, she worked hard to provide for her family, but the money never went far enough. Though she had the tiniest, least expensive apartment in the area, she struggled to pay the rent. She couldn't manage in one paycheck. It took most of both checks each month. It seemed she either had to buy food or gas for the car or pay the babysitter, or pay the rent. She couldn't manage many necessary things like shoes, and warm clothes, much less luxuries. Birthdays or Christmas would leave her so depressed. Many invited them for meals and gave gifts to the children so they'd feel loved on these special days. The ladies loved Annette and brought food and clothing to help. It always resulted in rejoicing over meeting this little family's need.

The MDW Chaplain, Colonel Syl Shannon, handsome, jovial, took the Ladies' Bible Class to his heart and was so thoughtful and supportive. One Christmas he had a big box of toys, which were used, but good, donated for needy children. After his program on base, which had distributed hundreds of these toys, this box full was left over. He called the Ladies' Bible Class to offer these "leftovers," if we could use them for any needy. Could we!!

We called Annette first and several other women who wouldn't have much for their little ones. She cried -- she hadn't been able to buy a single thing for either of the kids, and it was only a week till Christmas. She cried and then rejoiced over the doll for little Jessica and the game for John.

What a happy time as other ladies came in and selected some "gift from the Lord" for their children. Truly it was a blessing Jesus sent to us, through our thoughtful Chaplain. We could hardly wait to tell him all about it.

"We even had toys and dolls left over after our ladies had taken some gifts for their children," I told Chaplain Shannon. "So we sent

86

the rest with Pauline Hayes to give away at their little church, The Upper Room."

"That's wonderful!" he said, "I like to help those small churches."

There were other wonderful Chaplains who loved and encouraged the ladies, but this one really had a Shepherd's heart, and looked on us as "his lambs."

I want to add a storybook ending.

Annette met and married a handsome Christian widower. She's staying home and is the joyful mother of children Psalms 113 speaks about. They live happily ever after.

Chapter 25

FOLLOWING
GEORGE WASHINGTONS' EXAMPLE

We knew the exhortation in I Timothy 2:1-2 that "first of all, supplications, prayers, intercessions and giving of thanks, be made for all men; for kings, and for all that are in authority; that we might lead a quiet and peaceable life, in all godliness and honesty."

Our first duty then, should be to pray for everyone and especially for leaders, in order that we might have a Nation where we can lead a godly life.

George Washington was a man of prayer. <u>George Washington, the Christian</u>, written by William Johnson, contained 24 pages of beautiful prayers written by Washington when he was about twenty years old. The book of prayers, out of print for more than 50 years, is proof of George Washington's devotion to Jesus Christ. The prayers for guidance and forgiveness through the blood of Jesus Christ were not the words of a Deist! As President and Commanding General of the Continental Army, he was God's man, chosen for the time of America's greatest crisis. His disciplined prayer life undoubtedly affected the decisions of this great leader.

The Bible records the effects of a God-fearing King upon the nation of Israel which were peace, prosperity and blessings on the people. The effect upon America, of being governed by a God-fearing Christian President? We can't be sure until heaven's books are opened.

In his Inaugural Address, President George Washington spoke these words: "Smiles of Heaven can never be expected on a Nation that disregards the eternal rules of order and right, which Heaven itself has ordained." In his first official act, he prayed fervently to "that Almighty Being, who rules over the universe, who presides in the councils of nations...that His benediction may consecrate to the liberties and happiness of the people of the United States."

Following the example of George Washington, we also fervently pray, acknowledging our Heavenly Father, who indeed does rule over the universe and councils of nations, that He might restore America, helping her to return to Him as a Nation who does not disregard the eternal rules of order and right, which God Himself has ordained.

The first Prayer Breakfast in the Pentagon was begun by a few men, who had the desire of seeking a public gathering within the building, where we might corporately pray for our Nation and its leaders. The National Prayer Breakfast is now an annual event with the President and other dignitaries in attendance. We desired to have our own Prayer Breakfast coincide with this one.

The first planning meetings were held in Mr. John Broger's office, with Christian men in leadership and Mrs. Jean Davis and myself. We were asked to represent the Christian women of the Pentagon. Where could we hold it? How could we arrange for the President's speech to be "piped in?" What would we eat? Who would speak? Would we need music? If so, who would do it? Should we charge if we served food? Would anyone be willing to take leave to attend this kind of event? These and many other questions were put forth and we all agreed it was worth trying.

If we wanted to see our Nation turned back to godly principles and righteousness, we had to be intercessors. This was the burden on John Broger's heart, and we felt God had placed him in his job, to stir us up to fervently pray for our leaders in such a time as this. With no money, the handful of Christians began to pray that God would help us establish an event specifically for the purpose of praying for our great land and its leadership. What we lacked in numbers, we made up in enthusiasm.

The first Prayer Breakfast held on February 1, 1972, was mostly "in-house," with prayers and testimonies from men and women in the Pentagon Christian community. They exalted God's goodness and mercy to us and recalled America's beginnings and beseeched Him to once again let righteousness exalt our land and bring peace. It was informal, but well received. The President's speech at the National Prayer Breakfast was "piped in" for the Pentagon people. We joined him as he prayed for our servicemen in the Vietnam conflict.

Our Pentagon Prayer Breakfast was broadcast live over the Armed Forces Radio Network each year and heard throughout the world at American military bases. "I was in Vietnam and heard the Pentagon Prayer Breakfast live in my quarters," John Broger told me. "It's a small world."

Each year, the program has become more formal, with better planning. The MDW Chaplains have played an ever-increasing part in the Pentagon Prayer Breakfasts. Their support of this laymen's program has been invaluable. Chaplain Norman Walker thought of a new idea to make it more efficient, by selling tickets in advance and providing his staff assistance. Following George Washington's example, godly men in leadership of the military were asked to be our speakers for this annual event. Each year attendance has increased. Our private dining room has people standing and every chair filled. We continue to stress prayer as our reason to gather together. Prayer for our nation to remain free. Prayer that we would be what our money declares "one nation under God."

Each year the ladies of the Bible Classes and prayer groups have been supportive. Like the massive pillars in the building, they support, but they aren't really in the limelight. They agree they've been called to support the men in leadership, in any way they need help, without taking over their authority. Each year one woman is selected to represent all the Christian women in the building by reading a Scripture selection as part of the program. What a joy to be part of it, without all the responsibilities of leadership. God has given His women a restful position, as protected sisters, in the Pentagon Christian community.

There have been ten annual Pentagon Prayer Breakfasts. The program is timed so that attendance will require no more than one hour annual leave from busy staffers. True to military discipline, the program is promptly started and concluded which is nothing short of miraculous for the non-professionals who plan and prepare this service! The morning of the Breakfast, the Christian men and women arrive early and find their tables, where they serve as hosts and hostesses, welcoming the people and serving coffee and rolls. Generals and officers are interspersed with enlisted and civilians on a first-come seating basis. Everyone is introduced and prayer is order of the day.

"America! America! God shed His grace on thee..." opening strains of this familiar hymn focus our attention to the very reason for gathering! To seek God's blessing on America, to repent, and to pray for our government.

Guest speakers, bringing words of patriotism and rallying everyone to pray for our nation's leaders, have come from our own military leadership. Special music and soloists have been provided from the metropolitan area churches and military groups. Our gratitude goes to each of the following who have made each breakfast very special:

Prayer Breakfast Chairmen

John Broger organized and provided leadership for several years, arranging recording and broadcasts of it. Then Col. Jim Meredith, Col. Dick Miller, Bob Schneider, Bill Allison, Major Jerry Tiahrt, Lt. Col. Gene Cargile, Col. Al Husnian, Major Don Buchanan, Col. Jim Bennett and Captain Bruce Bell have assumed the responsibilities for oversight of our annual prayer gathering.

Chaplains

Although begun as a laymen's activity, the MDW staff Chaplains have served on the Committee for these Prayer Breakfasts and have become increasingly supportive. They have assumed responsibilities for posters, tickets and programs, providing a piano, and practical helps. Special thanks to MDW Staff Chaplains Assistant M/Sgt. Schonefeld and to Chaplain Cook, Chaplain Syl Shannon, Chaplain Ives, Chaplain Norman Walker, and Chaplain Cliff Weathers among many others whose names may have been overlooked, but recorded in heaven.

Guest Speakers

Rear Admiral John B. Johnson, Major General Louis Rachmeler, USA; Brigadier General Jerry R. Curry, USA; Major General Clay Buckingham, USA; Brigadier General Carl H. McNair, Jr., USA; General J. W. Vessey, Jr., USA; Rear Admiral Frank C. Collins, Jr., USN; and Jack Wyrtzen of the Word of Life Fellowship.

Special Music

Special music has been provided for these events by singers from the Washington Bible College, the Metropolitan Christian Center singers "New Creation," and a group of singers from the Evangel Temple Choir. In addition to these musicians we have had the fine talents of the military services, the US Navy Sea Chanters, the US Army Chorus, the USAF Singing Sergeants, and a soloist, S/Sgt. Ron Simmons of the US Marine Corps. We gratefully acknowledge these fine artists who have come and have made our program complete.

Special Thanks

We could not fail to mention the donation each year for all ten Prayer Breakfasts from the Pentagon Florist, who has made up a special fresh flower centerpiece for the head table. Immediately after the program, the centerpiece has been used on the altar at the noon devotional services sponsored by the MDW Chaplains and then given to the Secretary of Defense as a gift from the Prayer Breakfast Committee.

Perhaps history has been changed, in ways we may never know, because these people gave their time and energies to support a program of prayer in the Pentagon, following the example of our early leaders in America. These are real people who have blessed us.

There are voices rising all over the nation, demanding an end to prayer, and to separate...no, to eliminate God from the affairs of our government. This great nation was founded on freedom to worship God, and seek His Divine protection and guidance. Benjamin Franklin's speech at the Constitutional Convention in 1787 admonished the Delegates not to omit God, but to offer prayers every morning "imploring the assistance of Heaven and its blessing..." Franklin pointed out, "the longer I live, the more convincing proofs I see of this truth: that God governs in the affairs of man..."

History pages are full of instances where leaders' prayers were heard and answered. Following the example of early leaders in our nation, great men like George Washington, who acknowledged "God's wonder-working providences" they prayed. And we, like a Gideon's band, the small band of Christians in the Pentagon, gather together to pray.

"God bless America!" That is our prayer. May God once again have mercy on the affairs of the United States of America.

Chapter 26

WEINBERGER – A MAN OF PRAYER

How delighted we were to learn that Secretary of Defense Caspar Weinberger is a man of prayer himself! We found this out from an aide, Sergeant Mary Conyers, who attended our Bible Class. Everyone loved Mary. Her charming smile and enthusiasm for life bubbled over with "Praise the Lord!" Whether things were good or bad, Mary had a total confidence that God was in control, and would bring something beautiful out of it, just as He had done with her own life.

Mary invited the Ladies' Bible Class to her commissioning ceremony. Her family had come from the midwest for the big day. Her dad held the Bible as Mary took the oath. Secretary Weinberger himself read the citation and acclaimed her fine work for the Department of Defense. He asked Mary's mother to help pin on the new Lieutenant bars, "without personal injury."

Around a buffet table afterward, I had an opportunity to speak with Secretary Weinberger. I told him there were groups of employees who gathered daily in the building to pray for him and all our leaders.

"Thank you, I need it more than you know," he replied. "I'm a firm believer in prayer." He initiated questions about the devotional groups and spoke of the need our nation has for God's divine guidance and protection.

Secretary Weinberger is a soft-spoken, slightly smaller built man than you would expect for one carrying such weighty matters of national importance. What an honor and a pleasure it was to meet and talk with him!

A few months later, the attempted assassination of President Reagan brought to focus clearly, once again, the need for Christians to be on their knees in prayer daily, interceeding for God's blessings on our leaders.

Chapter 27

A CUP OF COLD WATER

Our Military Chaplains are busy men!

Most often the on-going leadership of the Pentagon devotional groups was held by civilians like John Broger, John Polansky, Homer Belle Isle, Russ Delaney, Bob Schneider, Bill Allison, Paul Brady, and Ernie Bockstanz, whose faithfulness over the years was inspiring.

Throughout the year, on National holidays and special occasions, religious services are regularly held at the Pentagon for all Department of Defense personnel. The Chaplains arrange for some prominent leaders to come, at their own expense, as a ministry to our military troops. In addition, many college and military choirs from the various Military Academies perform occasionally as a ministry to the Pentagon personnel.

Overflow crowds have jammed into the auditorium to hear "the Tramp for the Lord," Corrie ten Boom, and Colleen Townsend Evans, Billy Graham, Norman Vincent Peale, Keith Miller, Hal Lindsey, Bishop Fulton J. Sheen, Pat Robertson, Arthur Katz and many more famous men and women of God. All have come to bring words of encouragement, hope and love of country. We have been grateful and inspired by their ministry. Arranging for programs and speakers such as the ones mentioned, the MDW Staff Chaplains are truly bringing "a cup of cold water"...refreshing the troops, the men and women protecting our Nation stationed at the Pentagon.

In June 1976, Corrie ten Boom came to speak for the Pentagon Chaplains noon service. The huge auditorium was packed and this much-loved 84 year old "Tramp for the Lord" received a standing ovation. She was introduced by Secretary of the Navy, J. William Middendorf, who said he and his wife were acquainted with Corrie when he was serving as the U.S. Ambassador to the Netherlands. Corrie was instrumental in leading him to the Lord in 1971. Secretary Middendorf thanked John Broger and Chaplain Cook for arranging the program and Corrie's visit to the Pentagon, which he said had a greater spiritual awareness than any place he had visited in Washington or in the whole country.

"I've reached this building so often in my prayers," Corrie began, "because I know you are standing on the front lines of a terrific battle, perhaps the most serious and important battle in this place, where the battle between darkness and light is fought. Everyone knows that here everyone makes decisions that can and will influence the whole world. That is why it is such a joy that you have a book -- a book almost bursting with good news -- the Bible. Here God tells of His plan, and it is good when we are standing on the front line that we know the plan of the "Central staff." Corrie was breathless from the long walk across the building and up to the 5th floor.

"I hope when I speak you will understand a little bit, how important your life is here, in the Pentagon building, in America, in this world. We are in the midst of a battle, a real battle, more severe than has ever been in the history of the world. But God's logistics are perfect! We find that by reading the Bible we must study to see how rich we are."

"I used to tell people to keep looking up and kneeling down. Now I say keep looking down, from your position of victory on your problem, then you will see that you are also made more than conquerors. And we must march on."

"I want to share a little legend about the Lord Jesus' return to heaven. It has helped me very much. The angels gave Him a fantastic welcome and gathered around Him with many questions about what His death, resurrection and ascension was all about. Jesus replied "the redemption of the world."

"But you have come back here, how will the world know about it?" the angels asked Him.

"I have trained my men to evangelize the whole world. Yes indeed, every corner of it," Jesus told them.

"How many men did you train for such a mammoth task?" the angel asked.

"A handful," was Jesus reply.

The angels responded, "A handful? But what if they fail?"

"If they fail, I have no other plans!" Jesus told them.

"Is that not an awful risk to take?"

And Jesus replied, "No. They will not fail!"

"When He said that...He spoke about you who are here, who know the Lord Jesus and have given Him room in your life and in your heart that Jesus could come in. You stand on a victory place!" Corrie told us. "We stand on the front lines, but we stand on victory ground because Jesus was, is and will be Victor! And He has given us a tremendous task in this time, for in II Corinthians 5, we read 'we are Christ's ambassadors...'" do you realize that? That you are a representative from heaven on this earth? The Astronauts were representatives from the earth to the moon. Far more, when you are a child of God and you are a representative from heaven to this earth!'"

"How important is it? I have no reason to tell you, of all people, what an Ambassador is...you understand better than many people. You know that an Ambassador stands in authority of the one who sent him. And you and I stand in authority of Jesus Christ who has sent you and me to be the light of a very dark world.

"When I was in the concentration camp we had to sleep in a room that was built for 200 prisoners. We had to sleep with 700. People started to grumble and fight. If the guards found out there was fighting in our building, we all would have been punished in a cruel way and Betsie said "Corrie, let's pray," and she prayed and prayed and prayed. First there was shouting and swearing and bitter words and then it grew quieter and quieter and when at last all was quiet, Betsie said, "Thank You, Father. Amen."

"Do you see there, the tremendous work that was done? Betsie was the representative from heaven in that place of horror. If there had been ten righteous people in Sodom and Gomorah, then they would not have been destroyed. It is very important, that you are children of God, and that you are here in America, you are here in the world. There are people who live in a corner of the world and they have responsibilities for that little corner. But you are not in a corner...you are in the center of the whole world!"

"I like to pray with an open Bible. I like to say 'Father here you have said it, now you must do it.' It is so good to know that we can pray for each other, and I'm so glad to know that there are so many prayer groups here! God has said, very clearly, that we must pray for all who are in authority and we have to do that. Many people pray for you who work here!"

"I know that some of you are real prayer warriors. But some of you are not. You think 'that is nothing for me...' that 'it is good for him, or her, but I'm not a good prayer warrior.' Then I must tell you something. There was a little boy and he was saying 'A, B, C, D,...' and his mother said, 'What are you doing?' He replied 'I have never prayed before, but I was told I had to pray, so I told the Lord I was giving Him the whole alphabet and said 'God will you make a good prayer out of it?' That boy understood what we read in Romans 8 where it is written 'that the Holy Spirit himself teaches us to pray and prays in us.'"

"Not only do we have each other here, but there are people praying for you here in the Pentagon building and we have also many angels around us. There are angels here but we don't see them, we experience them. Sometimes I wish I could see them. Sometimes in the camp I said, 'It cannot be worse than today,' but the next day was worse. Then Betsie and I talked about Romans 8:18, "the suffering of this time is not worthy to be compared to the coming glory..." the best is yet to be! That is very encouraging and it can help someone who is in the battle, it is very important to remember that we are fighting a victorious fight. We need to remember the strength of our army...those that go with us are far more than those who are against us! And He that is in us is stronger than the whole world."

"How terribly sick is the world! Perhaps you know better than anyone else, because you stand here in the front lines, in the center, where you are fighting -- as it were -- for the whole world! Is there hope for the world? The Bible says that he who believes Jesus is the Son of God overcomes the world...you have to overcome the world."

"We have not to defend Jesus Christ and christianity. We have only to understand that we are in the offense! We do not fight as people who have to defend ourselves, for we know the secret of God's plan, it is this:"

"Are you afraid, when you read of what will happen to the world before Jesus returns? I understand it, for what we once could only read in the Bible we now can read in the newspapers and magazines! It is happening and we know that terrible things have happened and will happen. When you are scared, just look at the last page of the Bible and there we read that Jesus has promised that 'I will make everything new.' And this world will be covered with the knowledge of the Lord as the waters cover the sea. The best is yet to be! God hasn't given us a spirit of fear, but of love and a sound mind."

"I was in a concentration camp where 97,000 women were killed, or died, and I saw death in their eyes. I was surrounded with people who had training in cruelties and there I could say, with Paul, 'I count everything as loss, compared to the overwhelming privilege of knowing Jesus Christ and getting more intimately acquainted with Him.'"

"I saw the smoke of the Crematorium, I did not know that one week before they killed all the women of my age, I should be set free. God's love still stood."

"Oh, give yourselves totally to the Lord and don't make any more compromises. One day I talked with a high businessman and I said 'Do you go 100% with the Lord?' He said 95%. I told him 'You are bought with a high price, the precious blood of Jesus. You must give everything. Did you ever face death?' He said, 'Yes, I was in the war.' I asked him, 'When you knew you were facing death, did you give 95%?' He said, 'No, 100%.' I said 'Man, wake up to reality! Don't you understand that at this moment, we all stand before a Crematorium? In a world where there are Atomic Bombs in the hands of bad and stupid people? We must be ready! And we can be ready! We can go into battle without anything to fear.' And that businessman surrendered 100%. 'It will be difficult for me,' he said, 'but it doesn't matter.'"

"Some ask me, 'were you afraid, when you stood there, in front of the Crematorium?' I must ask you...afraid of what?

To fear the Spirit's glad release?
To pass from pain to perfect peace?
The strife and strain of life to cease?
Afraid of death?
Afraid of what?
Afraid to see the Saviour's face?
To hear His welcome? and to trace,
The glory beams from wounds of grace?
Afraid of death?
Afraid of what?"

Corrie concluded, "Let's pray. Thank You Lord! We have nothing to be afraid of, and that you give us the good logistics for life and for death. Turn our eyes in the right direction, unto Your victory. Lord, bless these people here, who are standing in the front line of the battle, who are standing in the center of the happenings in this world. And Lord when we look around we are distressed, when we look within we are depressed, but when we look at You, Jesus, we are at rest! So turn our eyes in the right direction! Through Your Holy Spirit, Hallellujah! Amen."

Chapter 28

WHAT HAPPENS
WHEN WOMEN PRAY?

Sounds like a good title for a book doesn't it? It is, or I'd have used it. So you can see I heartily agree with Evelyn Christensen that Great and Mighty things happen when just plain, ordinary women will pray a prayer of faith. This chapter will relate a few exciting instances where God has confirmed His Word, as two or three women agree in prayer for needs.

I hesitated to write this chapter. It isn't for our glory, but for magnifying the name of Jesus. We don't want any credit. We can't take any. We couldn't do anything by ourselves and we acknowledge "it is only His grace" to hear and answer that any of this came to pass. But these miracles did happen when we prayed.

Perhaps you might get discouraged reading these supernatural works of God, thinking "I never get my prayer answered" or "I prayed and God didn't heal me or my baby, etc." Yes, that does make me hesitate...but I feel it will increase your faith to know that God is willing and able to do exceedingly abundantly above all that you could ask or even think. Faith comes from hearing the word of God. These testimonies are results of acting on what the word of God said. I believe that faith will result from hearing and reading about what God has done.

Could we do what Jesus did, just because we were believers? He said we would do even more, but we rarely think it applies to us "ordinary women."

* * * *

Sometimes God has done miracles and we were astounded, just to be part of it. Dorothy Kennedy was shy and didn't speak much in our class, but one day she asked for prayer. She had a speech impediment, which made it difficult for her to answer the office phone. This upset her boss and others and embarrassed her. She was really concerned about keeping her job, since she was supposed to answer the phone as part of her duties. We'd never faced such a problem, but recalled the incident in Mark 7, where Jesus healed a man with such an ailment. He spit, touched the man's tongue and spoke healing. The man was instantly healed, and spoke plainly.

So we asked Dorothy if it would be alright, if one of us could touch her tongue and we'd all pray for this healing. She readily agreed. We did, and she spoke plainly, just as the young man in Mark did! All glory to the name of Jesus!

We're still praising God for this miracle we see and hear daily. If anyone comes now with a speech problem, we call on Dorothy to pray. We know she has faith!!

* * * *

Most miracles we think of are related to healing, but this one isn't. Yet, it was so thrilling. Pauline Hayes was a newlywed and the wife of a young Minister, Rufus Hayes, struggling to establish a tiny inner-city church. Finances were definitely tight, and no prospect in sight for any funds for clothing. She had worn her thread bare winter coat for years. She wanted a new coat, but didn't voice the desire, except to the women in the Pentagon Bible Class. We prayed God would supply the desire of her heart, without them going into debt and without her having to ask her husband, and make him feel inadequate to provide.

The next week, we entered the Meditation Room and there, on the table, was a brown grocery bag taped shut. Written on the outside was a message "A gift from Jesus." We'd never seen a bag there before and with such a message. We couldn't wait to open it! Inside was a coat. Not just an ordinary coat, it was black cashmere! Not only that it had a White Mink Collar. It didn't fit anyone...except Pauline! We laughed and clapped our hands and praised God for answering our prayers! And for doing more than we could even ask for.

* * * *

God had to make one man sicker, to answer our prayer for his healing. It wasn't what we had in mind! Lillian Whitmore had asked for prayer for a friend, who was to have his tongue cut out, as a result of cancer. The thought was so dreadful, to think he'd never be able to eat, nor talk again. It caused us to cry as we prayed we asked "for a miracle, that he wouldn't lose his tongue at all." He was scheduled for surgery that very day, when we prayed.

Almost fearful, dreading the worst, yet still clinging to the "prayer for a miracle," we inquired the next day as to the man's condition. "Oh, he's much worse," was the reply. Lillian said, "He started running a high fever yesterday and they had to postpone the surgery. They're giving him antibiotics."

Someone said "Praise the Lord!" Others didn't think there was much to praise the Lord for, and indeed it didn't look like it. He was sicker and sicker for two weeks.

Finally he improved and the Doctors x-rayed and prepared for the surgery, only to discover that they no longer needed to remove the tongue! They did cut out a tiny piece to "test" it. The cancer had disappeared.

* * * *

Major Jerry Tiahrt, USAF, was about to pin on his Lieutenant Colonel ensignia. He'd been assigned to the Pentagon after a varied and exciting career as a fighter pilot. It was the "pits!" His office was in the basement, no windows, noisy and he didn't even have a desk! He felt like many who are sent to the building, he hated it and took out his frustration on his family.

God used this miserable situation to draw Jerry to Him. He got saved and began coming to the morning devotions. He was as excited about the Lord as he'd been for things of the world. He began to devour the Bible and couldn't get enough of Jesus. He felt a burden for the singles in his church and he and Bonnie began a ministry to them. They opened their home for fellowship and teaching meetings. His teaching was so practical, we asked Jerry to come and share with our Ladies' Bible Class on dating, choosing a mate, and marriage. Jerry and Bonnie were guest speakers for many of our Retreats.

One year, Jerry accepted the leadership of our Pentagon Prayer Breakfast and did an outstanding job. His military job was going great too. He liked working for Major General Vandenberg. Then God opened a door and he felt God would have him resign his commission in the Air Force and help with a political campaign. No one could believe he'd give up benefits he'd worked for for 15 years! But the day before he was to pin on his Lieutenant Colonel rank, he resigned. When the campaign was over he was without a job and no prospects!

Jerry needed $800 to meet his bills. It was urgent. The ladies prayed. It looked impossible, but the day before it was due, the Tiahrt's received a cashier's check for $800, with no identification. There were many more prayers offered for Jerry and Bonnie during the next six months, while he looked for a job. God opened a door, by "creating" a job in Washington, DC with a salary increase above his Air Force pay! God was faithful during that six months of unemployment and money came from unknown people who wrote that "God had told them to send them money!" They never missed a payment or had a need unmet! What a miracle!

* * * *

Sometimes God answered and it didn't "look" like it, so we had to depend on His Word and not appearances or feelings. Such was the case when we prayed for Nan Word, who asked healing for her little toe. She had surgery on it once and it wasn't successful. The doctor said they would try again.

It was painful and she couldn't wear hardly anything, but a slipper. The toe stuck out almost 90° to her foot, it looked like it was broken and just sticking out at a right angle to the rest of her toes. We prayed God would heal without surgery, and after we finished, it looked the same, but it didn't hurt when she walked. We were delighted. The next day she wore a regular shoe! Her toe

100

simply didn't hurt anymore, though it didn't look much different than it had before we prayed.

She went to her podiatrist and he was as happy as she was. He said there was no need for surgery, if it didn't hurt her anymore. PTL! It never hurt her again! Praise the name of Jesus! But you couldn't tell by looking.

* * * *

When Alice Hall had asked for prayer for finances, it was really desperately needed. Her husband had been injured and out of work for about a year. We prayed and nothing changed. If anything it got worse! Alice had confidence that God would provide, but the days, weeks and months went by with bills mounting. We continued to pray.

One Wednesday, she said she "didn't know if she could take the pressure much longer." After class, she called home to check on the children when they came home from school. She asked about the mail, expecting more angry "overdue" notices.

There was a letter from the insurance company and she assumed it was more forms to be filled out, regarding the injury. She asked her daughter to open the letter. It contained a check for $10,000!

God's timing is never our timing, but He always comes through. After teaching us patience and faith.

* * * *

Cancer is something that everyone dreads to think about. Kathy White was no different. When she discovered a mole on her neck had enlarged, quite suddenly, and changed from brown to black, she was fearful of cancer.

"You'd better get to the doctor," her coworkers advised, "that's nothing to fool around with." But she didn't have a car and the doctors in her area had closed their offices by the time her bus pulled in at 6:30 p.m. She didn't know any local doctors, so she just called a skin specialist in the D.C. phone book. They were rather abrupt and "not taking new patients." She took that as a sign from the Lord, since she didn't have the money to spend on a doctor anyway.

She was new in our Bible Class and had just asked for prayer, without giving any details. But the next day, she gave every detail. It seems she got home that night and was getting ready for bed and praying for the problem, as she brushed her teeth. She stopped brushing and looked at the mole. Kathy just touched it with her hand and asked God "to remove it, in Jesus' name."

It fell off in her hand! She couldn't believe it. There was no scar, no spot, nothing to indicate that there had even been a mole there! At work the next morning, she told her coworkers about it and they were horrified. "That's really terrible, you'd better call the doctor right now," they advised.

101

She wondered if they were right, but she wanted to tell the Bible Class first. We rejoiced and praised God. So did she! God removed it without surgery and she's never had another problem with a mole, or cancer.

* * * *

Peggy Martinez was expecting her second baby any day. It was distressing for her to face the delivery, as she had such a difficult time with the first child. She asked for prayer, that God would help her and she wouldn't be fearful. She got bigger and more uncomfortable, as the baby was overdue. She kept working, so her leave would stretch as much as possible. They needed her income, while she'd be off on maternity leave. We prayed for her every day, and she never missed a Bible class in the morning or at noon.

One Thursday she wasn't in class at noon, and before we ended, we prayed for Peggy. That was about 12:50. I had a phone call at 2:30 that afternoon from Peggy. She was so apologetic, "I hated to call you at the office, Nita, but I wanted you to know that I had my baby."

"When did it happen? You were in class this morning and felt okay," I said. "Well, about 10 o'clock I didn't feel so good and by 11, I decided to call my husband to come and get me. Pablo couldn't get there until 12 o'clock, but drove me right to the hospital. I had the baby at 1 o'clock," Peggy told me. "It was the easiest delivery anyone could ever have. I just didn't hardly have any pain at all, and I knew you girls were praying for me, while I was having my little Angela." God did do a whole lot more than we could have asked! But we asked!

* * * *

We've prayed for a lot of back problems over the years. Some long lasting, recurring types, some resulting from injury...God was no respector of persons. He healed them all! But, not all in the same way.

Nan Word came into the class one noon, bent over with pain. She was on the way to the doctor at that very time, because of her back pain. Only it hurt so bad she didn't think she could make it down the stairs to the bus. She had stopped in for prayer. We all gathered round her and laid hands on her and prayed. While we prayed she said she "felt her back get warm and then hot." By the time we finished she had no more pain!

She was astounded and we agreed that it was a real miracle! However, she felt she had better go to the doctors office and keep her appointment since he was expecting her. So she did go and told him what had happened when we prayed. Whether he believed it or not, she didn't know. He laughed when she told him she thought she should keep her appointment, even though she was feeling fine!

* * * *

102

Susie Ezzell needed prayer for pain in her back, which was so intense and sharp she could hardly walk. We prayed and she prayed, but it got worse. Finally her doctor recommended a specialist and surgery was scheduled. We still prayed for a miracle without it, but God chose to heal her through this method. Her healing was rapid and complete and she gave God all the glory. She kept in touch with other patients, who shared her hospital room and found many still suffered pain, long after their surgery.

God answered our prayer, but why didn't He do it the same for both women? We don't know, but we know His ways are perfect and He loved them both and made them whole again.

* * * *

Psoriasis is so ugly and a pretty young woman was self-conscious because of it on her feet and legs. "I've had it all my life," she told us.

"But Jesus can heal that, if you want us to pray for you," we enthusiastically told her, and she agreed we should lay hands on her. She was embarrassed, when we laid our hands right on her legs and feet to pray. But Jesus had touched the Leper in an act of compassion, and we knew He wouldn't hesitate to touch her skin problem, nor should we.

We prayed and nothing apparently happened. We forgot about it.

Several months later she came into class beaming and asked how we liked her new shoes? "I've never been able to wear sandals before because of my Psoriasis. But now that it's gone I have my first pair of pretty shoes."

We had forgotten about our prayer, but God hadn't. "He had worked it ever so slowly," she told us, "and it just began to gradually get lighter and more pale and disappeared." Praise Jesus!

* * * *

With so many people wanting abortions these days and cases of child abuse and neglect, it was refreshing to have some of the women ask for prayer to get pregnant. Most of these ladies had been married a long time and had tried everything the medical profession could suggest. But they knew God made barren women into joyful mothers, so we prayed for that blessing.

One recent case was Bobbie Gaines. We had prayed about her desire to have a baby and also about a job she'd applied for. Well...she got the job and we rejoiced. She loved it! Shortly after she began working, she got sick and she seemed to stay sick. She went to the doctor, who confirmed that she was indeed pregnant! She cried, but with joy, "God answered, before we prayed...while we were praying, I was already that way."

God is so good, isn't He? There is nothing too big, nor too little, to concern Him...and He wants to give us the desire of our hearts.

* * * *

103

I couldn't miss a chance to share my own testimony, could I? May it encourage your faith.

"You've got to have this oral surgery immediately, or you will lose your teeth." The words of the dentist overwhelmed me! It was such an unexpected announcement, I felt stunned.

"Does this condition ever get better?" I asked.

"No."

"Does it ever stay the same?" I questioned.

"Never," was his reply. It was so final and so urgent.

"Do you believe in miracles, doctor?" I almost hesitated to go that far by faith.

"Only if I can see one," he replied.

"Well, hang onto the x-rays, and you will," I told him. "I'm going to pray about it, wait for six months, and give God a chance before I try anything else."

He was a long-time acquaintance, our family dentist for over 15 years. His eyes filled with tears, "I don't want you to lose your teeth."

"Neither do I," was my reply. I may not have looked like I was scared when I walked out to meet my husband in the waiting room, but I was.

"That didn't take long," he said.

"No, it didn't," I replied. "Honey, it's your turn."

I sat praying, while he had his check-up, and as we drove back to work I told him the news and my decision. "You'd better get the elders to anoint you and pray for you tonight," he suggested, and I was eager to do everything I could to bring about a miracle in my mouth!

The elders prayed. I brushed and flossed faithfully, but I knew I couldn't heal the damaged bone that lay under the gums, nor heal the infection in the gum tissue...and nothing looked different. I fasted and prayed and asked others to pray as the day approached to return for my six month check-up. He looked me over with a fine-toothed comb, digging and gouging in every crevice! It felt like he was creating a few new cavities himself! Finally he turned off the overhead spotlight.

"I can't do anything else for you," he said.

He always cleaned our teeth, every six months, it was just automatic...and he hadn't cleaned my teeth! He had just studied the x-rays and dug around the teeth and gums, examining them.

"What do you mean, doctor?" I managed to ask, expecting the worst, by then.

"You don't need anything for another six months!" He told me.

I almost lept out of the chair. "Praise the Lord," I said, "it's a miracle."

"No," he replied, "it isn't a miracle."

"But you said the gum disease never got better, nor did it ever remain just the same -- and it has," I reminded him.

"It won't be a miracle," he emphatically informed me, "until the bone is restored."

104

That was ten years ago, 1972. We continued to go to that dentist until he retired. Then we were forced to find a new one. I wondered what his comments would be about my teeth and gums. For God had done a noteable miracle, and maybe more than one. I hadn't needed a filling during that entire period of ten years...which was remarkable, for someone who normally had several each time she went!!

"You have good teeth, and your gums are in excellent condition," the Hygenist told me, after she completed the cleaning. "Thank you," I said. I just didn't feel like explaining what had happened to me. Who would believe it? It almost seems like a dream to me now. When I was in the dentist's chair, he x-rayed and examined my teeth and mouth. "Your gums are in good shape, that's unusual for someone your age," he told me. I told him that the Lord had healed them. He was delighted, too, and he exclaimed, "Praise the Lord!"

* * * *

Another challenge to believe God occured.

"The doctor says I need to have a biopsy," Frances Mann told us in class one noon day. "If I have it done, I must sign a release that they can do a mastectomy if it's malignant. It scares me to death," she continued, "and I want you girls to pray." We did. We all dearly loved Frances! She had come to our Bible classes and the monthly luncheons for over two years. She had a delightful sense of humor and so much love for everyone she met. No one could resist that love! There had been tremendous growth over the period she had been coming to the Bible classes, and Frances was the first one to tell it.

"Friends," she would say, "I didn't know anything about the Bible till I came to this class, not that I know very much now," and she would chuckle, "but I know God answers our prayers, and the Bible is true."

Once a new lady had come, with questions, on "how to be sure if you were saved or not." After explaining and reading scriptures, I asked if she'd like to repeat a prayer after me, just to confirm her faith in Jesus blood atoning for her sins and to invite Him into her life as Lrd. She said "yes," but before I could speak, Frances spoke up. "Nita," she said, "couldn't we all repeat that prayer? There are some of us here, who haven't ever done it either, and we want to be sure we have met God's requirements for eternal life, too!" Their names were added to the Book of Life that day. PTL!

The child-like confidence Frances had, in God's ability to perform whatever He had promised, came about as a result of God instantly healing a bone spur. It had caused Frances much pain as she walked to her 5th floor office during the day. That healing encouraged her to believe God for miracles. We prayed and God immediately took the pain. You can imagine the joy we all felt as we returned to our desks after these noon prayer meetings!!

Back to Frances and the breast tumor -- She decided to see another specialist and get a second opinion. He told her the same thing, she needed to have the tumor removed and a mastectomy, if it was cancer.

105

"Well, Doctor," she told him, "I'm too old to fool around with something like this, but I'm not going to have the surgery. I am going to pray about it. I'M GOING TO THE GREATEST PHYSICIAN OF THEM ALL. I believe God can take care of this little thing, without all those mutilations." To her amazement, he said that he felt she was doing the right thing! He went on to say that there were some new theories that it wasn't always necessary, for women to have that drastic operation."

She made an appointment to return for a check-up in three months. The tumor was still there! Six months went by -- the tumor remained -- but her faith was unshakeable. The months turned to a year and the area was sometimes tender where that stubborn tumor lodged. Upon examining her the doctor asked if she had changed her mind and wanted the operation?

She replied, "Doctor, I'm just ignoring that old lump. The devil himself wants me to be worried, but I have got a lot of faith in God answering prayers from that little group of ladies in the Pentagon. He's not going to let them down and hurt their faith."

At one of our Retreats, about two years after she retired, Frances told us, "I just got so busy down at the Church helping all those poor people who were sleeping in the streets and encouraging them to fix themselves up and show the world what nice men and women they really were. Well, I just forgot about the lump! Then one day as I was dressing, I realized it was gone! I don't know when it happened, but I hadn't thanked the Lord," she concluded, "and I want to do that, here today, and thank you girls, for your prayers."

Hebrews 6:12 came to pass "with much patience and faith," she inherited the promise.

* * * *

Alcohol, cigarettes, drugs -- we had women come who needed to be set free from all these things. Jesus was the answer. He said "he had come to set the captives free," and He did.

"I'd like prayer," Jean Dawkins said, "that I won't be sick and suffer. I have decided that I want to give up my drinking and smoking, now that I have accepted the Lord." She continued, "My friends told me that I shouldn't give up everything at one time because it would make me sick and I would really suffer."

We prayed and she never wanted those things again, nor was she ill. Her hearty laugh and loving ways endeared her to everyone, and she was determined to walk with Jesus. She didn't miss a class, just like "old faithful" she was always there.

* * * *

Tilly Fowler shared her testimony with the class of how Jesus had set her free from her drug and drinking habits when she was saved. It was hard to believe that refined, beautiful, black lady was ever tipsy in her life!

Tilly became one of the leaders in the Bible Class Council Ring. She loves to play her harp and sing songs about Jesus. She wants to

106

be as enthusiastic for Him as she had been for the world. And she is!

* * * *

"I am always grateful for a few minutes to come into the class," Chris Plunkett said. "I always leave refreshed and encouraged. Sometimes the stress in the office is terrible and it's easy to be irritable with your coworkers, especially when the deadlines and work seem impossible to do." Rachel Young agreed, "We are so grateful for Christian sisters to pray with and encourage us! It is practical help too, it's the peace that the world can't give and the world can't take away!"

* * * *

I never get bored of testimonies of God supplying answers for small or big needs...I could write another book! But I have saved one of the best answers to prayer until now. A young woman, June Hendricks had a prayer request when she came, as many of us did.

"I have to go into the hospital tomorrow," June told us. "I'm scheduled for surgery the next morning for this goiter." Loosening a scarf from around her neck, she revealed the growth. It was large and looked like a small balloon was under her skin.

"The doctor tried to treat it for over a year with drugs, but it didn't work. So I must have the surgery -- unless the Lord heals me," June said.

"Do you believe the Lord can heal you? I asked.

"Oh, yes, I do," she said through her tears.

"All right, ladies, let's gather 'round and pray. I want everyone to lay hands on the sick just like Jesus said," I instructed them. I stood behind her and put my hands right on the bulging neck and we began to pray. We had hardly begun when the goiter began to shrink! I could hardly pray when I felt that mass moving underneath my touch! I got so excited! The ladies just continued to pray, but I was ready to shout for joy! Could she tell it was happening, too? As soon as there was a little pause, between women praying, I interrupted. "Jesus is healing her, right now! The goiter is shrinking while we've been praying! It's so exciting! June, can you feel it, too?" I asked.

"I could feel my neck getting warm and then hot, while you were praying," she said, and she reached up to feel her neck. "It is smaller! Oh, I think it's gone!! Oh, can you see it? Can you tell if it's gone?" She asked a dozen questions at once.

The ladies were so excited. They were dancing up and down and "Thank You, Jesus" was being chorused all over the room. "What a mighty God we have!" Jean Johnson said. It expressed perfectly our ladies' feelings as we left to go back to our offices after a thrilling lunch break.

The next week, June was back in class to give the report of what had happened after our prayers. She did go to the doctor's office, and he examined her and said that the goiter had shrunk and there was

107

no need for surgery. He was simply unable to explain it. It didn't change what God had done! "Facts are facts, whether a person believes them or not, they don't change," she told the class, "my healing is a fact, and I want to give God all the glory, and thank you for praying."

Would we ever doubt that God could heal anything? He is the same, yesterday, today and forever!

* * * *

God showed He was interested in everything that concerned us, even small things. Bobbie Harrison cashiered in the GPO BOokstore in the Pentagon. One evening as she checked out, prior to closing, she came out $1.00 over the amount she should have had. Her supervisor told her to recheck it the next morning and not to worry. She really felt bad about it. She didn't want to overcharge anyone. She prayed that evening and asked God to show her where she'd made a mistake and she asked His forgiveness. She knew it was her fault because she normally prayed each morning that God would help her not to make any mistakes during the day. This particular day she had forgotten to pray. God let her see she needed His help every day!

While she was still praying, God spoke to her and said, "the dollar is in the wrong drawer, it belongs in the Petty Cash drawer." She couldn't wait to get to work the next morning. Sure enough when she counted out the money, there was $99.00 in the drawer, instead of the $100 that should have been in it! She rejoiced and so did we, that God knew all about the money. We thanked Him also that she hadn't overcharged anyone.

* * * *

Alice Hall asked for prayer for her daughter, who was very sensitive about her appearance and embarrassed because of her teeth. "They have big spaces between the teeth," Alice said, "and the dentist said she needs braces, but I just can't afford it. Please pray with me that God will provide for this need." We prayed and time passed and most of us forgot about the need, until Alice shared this answer to prayer with the ladies.

"You remember I asked for prayer about my daughter's teeth? That was last August and at Christmas time I remarked that I thought her teeth looked like they were closer together. My daughter agreed that she thought so, too. Just over a month passed and now her teeth are perfect! There is no space or gaps between them at all!"

"Praise God!" Ruby Phillips exclaimed. Ann Gillenwater clapped with delight and all the women rejoiced over this miracle showing us once again of God's concern for us.

* * * *

Marie Yates shared how God gave her courage to witness to a General and his wife, with life-changing results.

108

"I was terrified!" Marie told us, "I had never ministered to anyone and I had a call from the 700 Club, telling me that I was the one to minister to Lieutenant General Richard Shaefer and his wife, Caroline." Marie continued, "With the encouragement of my husband, Bud, and the prayers of the Pentagon Ladies' Bible Class, I dropped tapes and books by their home every few days. I suggested they attend Kay Colville's Bible study and other meetings in the area, but I was amazed at the way they devoured the tapes! It was a miracle! Today Dick and Caroline Shaefer are in full time ministry, traveling all over the world. Both say that the teaching they heard on the tapes completely turned their way of thinking around. These same tapes led to their daughter, Lisa, who came to visit them, in accepting the Lord as well!"

Marie concluded, "My friend, General Jerry Curry, once told me, "When the Lord calls, our job is to 'Suit up and go...The Lord will do the rest'!"

* * * *

Sandi Gildea had asked the women to pray for a car for her son, who needed transportation to get to a new job. Sandi wanted to be sure she got a good car and not a "lemon" she couldn't afford to repair. Sandi went shopping that week and returned with the astounding report that one salesman turned out to be a Christian and he laid hands on the car and paryed for it to be perfect for her! Needless to say, Sandi bought that car! But her son didn't take responsibility for he car and worried Sandi when he stayed out too long with his friends. When he came home she told him that God was going to take care of the situation, since she was a widow and there was no Father in the home to correct him. Within two weeks the car was stolen! The son repented for his actions and after several weeks the car was found and the insurance company fixed up the car as good as new!

"The only way to deal with teenagers is through the Holy Spirit," Sandi says, "and God's Word. Just turn them over to God. You need to start your children very young, coming together to study the Bible. It isn't easily accepted and they rebel against restrictions, but the conviction of the Holy Spirit will break their rebellious spirit so they can say, "I'm sorry."

* * * *

Elaine Hedlund had asked prayer for finding just the right church where her husband would be happy. They tried a number of churches, but he got discouraged and just stopped going. We kept praying but before God answered our prayers, Elaine and Keith moved to San Antonio! Not long after they settled into their new home, Elaine wrote that they had found a wonderful church and they all just loved it and hadn't missed a Sunday! Besides that, God had directed Elaine to a noontime Bible study class at her new place of employment!

109

* * * *

Dottie Powell asked for prayer for God to provide a new suit for her son, which he needed for school. Her funds were limited and she shopped and shopped, without success. Time was getting short and he needed it quickly, so Dottie went back to one of the stores where she had already looked, just in case she had overlooked anything. There she found a beautiful brown suit, just her son's size! It was not on the right rack and was pushed towards the back, but there it was, just what she was looking for. When she pulled out the price tag she could hardly believe her eyes! That beautiful suit was marked down several times and was less than $20.00, which was all the money she had. We rejoiced that God knew her needs and provided.

"Life is exciting! There is never a dull moment when women pray!" Lieutenant Gwendolyn Fayne exclaimed!

I urge you to start praying today and see God work in your life too! In the name of Jesus, He will!

Chapter 29

LAYING HANDS ON SICK MACHINES

God proved that He was interested in everything we needed in very practical ways.

Suzie Ezzell had stacks of work, piled high, and most of it was urgent. When she arrived at work one morning, she found that her computer word processor wouldn't work! She did everything the manual said to do, and the only thing left was to call the service man. That usually took a day. She was desperate and prayed for God's help.

Then she recalled hearing of someone who'd laid hands on their car, and God had fixed it, so they could get home. Would He do it for her? Although she felt very foolish, she decided that she had to give God a chance to do it again. Her prayer was brief. She wondered if anyone saw her? She'd just have to tell them about the man's car, if they asked. She sat down at the machine and timidly pushed the "on" button. It whirred into action!

Suzie could hardly believe her eyes, but she began to type and people began to gather around. They all asked what she had done, because they all knew the machine was broken. Suzie had asked everyone, prior to this, to see if they knew anything to do to fix it.

She had an exciting morning, telling people that God had fixed her machine after she had prayed for it. Whether they believed it or not, they could see the machine worked. And work it did! All to the glory of the Lord.

Another sick machine:

The big Itek Camera wasn't working in my office. It was a really busy day and we had lots of briefing charts, graphs, maps and illustrations to photograph for our presentations.

My boss was doing his best to get the kinks out of that big machine, and take care of Project Officers as they came in with their work requests. Our Photographer, Cecil Webb, was on vacation and we really missed him. He had the magic touch it seemed, and kept our photo lab functioning when he was around. I later found out that Cecil prayed over the equipment, too!

My boss -- poor guy, he had worked so hard on that Camera. He had done everything. Twice. Still it wouldn't work. I had been concerned and prayed God would help him to repair the Camera, but it didn't seem like God was going to answer. I hesitated to say much about praying as he seemed to feel the Pentagon was no place to pray. Hours went by. Finally I took a break and walked into the photo lab to ask how he was doing.

"Gee, you've worked so hard on this machine all day," I said, "have you figured out what is wrong?"

"The timing mechanism is fouled up," he told me, shaking his head.

"You know, the Lord could fix this machine," I said. I laid my hand on the big camera. "I'm just going to pray," I kept my eyes wide open as I continued, "in the name of Jesus, and ask Him to."

"Well, nothing else has worked," he replied.

I went back to my desk and left him alone with the Itek Camera. In a few seconds I heard the machine whir into action! My boss came to the door, wiping his hands and smiling ear to ear. "Praise the Lord," I told myself.

"Nita," he told me, "we'd make a good team! You do the praying and I'll do the fixing."

I knew the angels had come to my rescue! In an emergency they had been sent to answer my cry for help.

Chapter 30

ANGELS TO THE RESCUE

Hebrews 2:14 says the Angels are sent to help those who will inherit the Kingdom. We know they do! However, God is practical. He doesn't tie our shoes or bathe us, but when we desperately need help and can't do any more for ourselves, He sends "heavenly helpers" to our rescue. I want to share a couple of such incidents.

* * * *

Kay Reynolds bubbled with excitement, as she entered the Meditation Room. "I've only got five minutes! I've got to rush back to the office," she gasped for breath. She had literally run to get to the prayer group. "I had to come and tell you what happened. It was a miracle! Really it was three miracles. You won't believe it...oh yes, you will, ha, ha."

She continued, "You remember I asked for prayer last Wednesday about my helping Karen and Jimmy pack to move. They were taking those adorable grandbabies to Corpus Christi." Kay told the ladies the rapid-fire events. Since they didn't have storage space, she brought back some of their things in her tiny Volkswagon, and returned home from New Jersey. She piled food, two Parakeet cages (complete with birds), and a baby buggy and a fish tank. It wouldn't all fit inside, so Jim had tied some of it on her VW roof.

It was raining as she started back to Virginia, and she knew we needed it, but she prayed, "Lord, let it stop raining long enough so I can unload the car and the birdies won't get wet." When she arrived at her youngest daughter, Kathy's apartment, she realized it suddenly stopped raining. It had poured all the way from New Jersey! "Thank you, Jesus," Kay uttered as she got out of the car. She knew, almost immediately, when she looked at the things tied on top of the VW roof, that she wouldn't be able to get the things off the luggage rack by herself. She looked around, but no one was to be seen.

"Help, Lord! I can't do this alone." She cried a quick plea. She turned back to inspect how her son-in-law, Jimmy, had tied the fish tank on the car. She couldn't figure out how to untie it, much less move it. She sensed someone's presence, and turned her head. A nice looking young man was coming up the walk. She was so desperate for help, she asked this stranger if he would mind helping her get the stuff off the roof of the car.

He not only didn't mind, he even carried it into the apartment for her! And then off he went. He disappeared so quickly from sight she didn't even see where he had gone.

What a miracle!

She hadn't even introduced herself or asked him his name. She had hardly even thanked him -- it all happened so quickly!

"It must have been an angel, sent to help you," some of the women voiced.

"I thought the same thing," Kay nodded, "but there is more..." After unloading the heavy fish tank and the bird cages at Kathy's place, she headed to her own home. When Kay got on the highway again, the rain began, hard. Kay was so thrilled over the answer to prayer, she never thought to pray for anything else.

However, when she arrived home she realized it wasn't raining there! Without getting wet, she unloaded all the groceries and the baby buggy. All the while she did, she was rejoicing over God's blessings. He had done exceedingly, abundantly more than she could even ask or think!

With exciting, fresh testimonies like this to stir up our faith, can you see why these Pentagon women would rather pray than eat?

* * * *

Now let me tell you about Marge, who had a very different need.

Marge had been in the Pentagon since 1942, before the building was completed. When her office moved into the building, they were still pouring concrete on the floor above her head! Marge was a disabled veteran, injured in World War II. She served in high-level Air Force staff offices, until she retired and was recently awarded the Meritorious Civilian Service Award at the ceremony honoring her 40 years service.

Marge wasn't able to make it to many of the Bible Classes, but faithfully attended the ladies' monthly luncheons, serving as Chairman in 1976. "Maybe now I'll be able to get to the Wednesday Bible classes," Marge said before she retired.

This attractive redhead, Marge Enright, had asked for prayer for her mother, who was 85 years old and had heart problems. She was in the hospital for weeks and then in a rest home for several months. She wanted to go home, which meant Marge would have to take care of her and continue her full-time job in the Pentagon. "Mother says those old people make her nervous," Marge chuckled as she told us, "she doesn't seem to realize she is old, too! Pray for us. I'm bringing her home next week." We prayed. Everyone loved Marge.

After a few weeks at home, Marge's Mom was much happier, but Marge was concerned that she wasn't doing enough to care for her. She got down on her knees and prayed, asking God to show her if there was something else she should be doing for her Mom. While she was praying, someone patted her on the head. Marge was startled. She looked up and then around the room, but no one was there.

She cried as she told us about it. "God really comforted me. It was as if His pat of approval was assuring me I was doing fine." Whether it was a pat on the head, or a helping hand, the angels had come to minister to a saint.

* * * *

We had numerous incidents of supernatural protection and help, and we knew the Angels were busy looking after us, but I want to relate something "different." It's about Lisa's Angel.

"We must judge angels? How could we? Why would we? Aren't they perfect?

These and many other questions came up in our class occasionally and I didn't know the answers. But I told the ladies that we would do it, because God had said we would. Even though I didn't understand it, I didn't doubt it, it was settled in heaven long ago, whether we understood or not!

Then something happened which gave me a little insight, perhaps, to a future event.

My niece, Lisa, had two miscarriages and it appeared as though she wouldn't be able to carry her third baby full term, but she did. A beautiful baby boy was born and happy parents had named him Nathaniel.

"The baby lived ten minutes," my sister, Hazel, told me on the phone. "Do pray for Gary and Lisa. They are so broken up over this loss. He was a perfect baby. They don't know yet what happened." We couldn't understand it. Why had God allowed her to deliver this baby and then take it so quickly? Although I acknowledged that He could bring something good, even out of tragedy. That night I prayed and asked God "Why?"

I had a dream that night. I want to share it with you. It comforted my heart and I'm praying it will touch yours, too.

I dreamed I was in heaven. I'd never had a dream of heaven, but I knew that was where I was. I stood before a throne, although I wasn't facing it. I was facing a long line of angels! As far as you could see...angels were lined up before the throne, waiting for something.

"You must judge this angel," the voice from the throne of God told me. And then it was read aloud from a book, that this angel had let Lisa's baby die!

When this report was read, the angel began to cry. "I didn't mean to do it," he said, "I just looked away for a minute. I just looked away for a minute and it happened." I began to cry, too. I understood how he felt.

"I can't judge this angel," I said, through my tears.

"You must judge this angel," God's voice was firm. There was no getting out of it.

"I judge him not guilty." My tears were flowing and I choked with emotion as I thought of his making a "mistake," just like we humans might do. I couldn't condemn him for something like that.

I've been forgiven for so much worse, how could I ever not forgive him?

My dream ended.

I woke immediately. There were real tears on my pillow.

Yet it comforted my heart to know that God hadn't planned to take that tiny baby, but had allowed it to happen, perhaps to give us a chance to show mercy, as we had received it from Him.

Chapter 31

FIRE !

One weekend early in January 1976, fire roared through a small portion of the building. The "PDQ" cafeteria corridor caught the brunt of the damage. Two months prior to the fire, the ladies in the Bible Class wrote a letter and had objected to the name selected for the quick service facility. We expressed in the letter to the DOD Concessions Manager, we didn't think it was appropriate to name a place using a curse word, even in an abbreviation known by everyone. We acknowledged their desire to convey quick service and fast food by the name and we offered, as substitutes, several names including "Quick-pik," and "Minuteman."

No reply. Finally Nancy Beauchesne went to see the Concessions Manager. "We couldn't answer, as you had no address on your letter! But," he said, "they couldn't possibly consider changing the name because of all the money invested in redecorating and painting the walls and name on the outside."

"Too late to change," they said.

Two days later, the fire gutted the ready to open "PDQ" facilities. We weren't surprised! God had given them opportunity to change! Nearly two months later the cafeteria was opened. This time the name was "Pentagon Pik-Quik."

The fire had been intense, resulting in much smoke damage. The hallways were like pitch black tunnels. In the strickened area there were few functioning lights, or darkened windows, to guide the hardy occupants who reported for work that Monday morning. The smell of smoke was so strong that some offices were unusable. Others were fouled from water damage, or a combination of both.

The firefighters deserved a great deal of credit for containing the fire in a small area of the building. The smoke billowed up stairways and along corridors, damaging valuable collections of military paintings on display. But the Pentagon spirit of dedication to our country prevailed and work went on. People shared offices and made-do. The teamwork and cooperation were fabulous.

With all the classified work involved and security precautions,

117

few details were released as to the cause of the fire nor the extent of the damage, just lots of rumors. The Ladies' Prayer Group just praised the Lord that God had kept the building operational, no deaths, etc., which could well have resulted, if the fire had taken place on a weekday. And a small miracle had occurred. The tiny Meditation Room had been spared from smoke, fire or water damage. Though the power was off and we couldn't meet there for several mornings, that little room had been protected and didn't even smell of smoke! This was unbelievable since surrounding corridors and offices were overpowered with the nauseating smoke odor and sooty black film. We knew the angels had been at work keeping our little haven available.

We prayed daily for our leaders and for God to protect our building and its occupants from the demonstrators, sabotage, and traitors from within who, like Judas, for a few pieces of silver turned on their friends and helped their enemies. The bomb threats had to be taken seriously, you could never be sure if they were real or a hoax. We prayed that God would send the angels to minister to these needs and help us. They surely came through this time! How many times had angels helped us that we weren't aware of?

Chapter 32

SECRET THINGS BELONG TO GOD

I was desperate! My husband, Bill, was out of town and we needed to get into our storage shed. That would have been easy, but I didn't have the key!

Our sons, Lew and Steve, were both attending Clemson University and away from home, except for a holiday visit. It was Thanksgiving weekend, and we'd had a wonderful time together. Bill had headed to western Maryland for his annual Deer hunting safari.

Lew needed to get something from our shed and, before Bill left, I forgot to ask where he kept the key. I never needed it before and it had been one of those things Bill took care of. So we searched the work room and everywhere, trying an assortment of keys. None worked.

"I could try a can opener or pry the door open, Mom," Lew volunteered.

"Oh, no! Bill would be furious," I replied. "I'll look on his dresser."

It wasn't there.

Before he left, Bill told Lew the item he needed to take back to college was in the shed, and I'm sure he thought no more about it. Neither did I, until now. It was almost time for them to go! What could I do? We had no phone at our isolated hunting cabin, and no neighbors within miles.

At last -- I thought to pray! Why hadn't I done it sooner? I felt guilty. I had tried everything before I turned to God, my heavenly Father, who had shown His love and willingness to help me so often. I had forgotten Him.

I dropped to my knees beside my bed, and asked God's forgiveness. "Without Me, you can do nothing," Jesus said, and He had let me learn that once again. Would I ever learn? I was ashamed. I prayed and asked the Lord to show me where the key was, and while I was asking, I had a vision. I wasn't asleep, but there I saw, just like in a dream, exactly where the key was located!

I saw an area in our laundry room, where we had a section of steel shelving. There was the key, hidden from view, hanging on a bent paper clip, which was attached to one of the front support braces.

I would never have found it. All you could see was a tiny piece of the paper clip, outside one of a multitude of holes in the steel brace.

"Thank You, Jesus," I joyfully exclaimed, as I got off my knees and rushed to the basement laundry room. Sure enough, there was the key, hanging on the clip just as I had seen it in the vision. I still couldn't see it, but I felt behind the brace and grabbed the key.

"The angels sure came to our rescue," Lew said, as he turned the key in the storage shed lock, "just in the nick of time."

"That was really neat, Mom," Steve told me, "now show us where that paper clip is, so we don't go through this again."

I'll never forget it, that unique answer to prayer. I'm quick to urge others to pray and ask God to help when they have a "lost" item.

"The angels know where it is," Bonnie Guiess told us in our Ladies' Bible Class recently. "Ask God to send them to minister to you." Bonnie was talking about bombs in the Pentagon, but I was recalling something as tiny as a key.

God wants to help -- He says ask and you shall receive. Remember, the Bible says "the secret things belong to God."

Chapter 33

MUSTARD SEED FAITH

"This tree has got to go," Bill told me after the air condition-er man left. They had made a pre-installation inspection and indicated the best position for locating the big compressor unit was right where our big Dogwood tree stood.

"Oh, Honey, it's such a pretty tree, couldn't you have them put the compressor somewhere else?" I asked. He explained their reasons for this location and it was final.

"Could you transplant the tree to the back yard? I'd rather have it there anyway." Again Bill's response was negative. "It was too big to move." So I accepted the inevitable.

Until that night.

Lying in bed, I got to thinking about having faith, to move mountains only requires the equivalent of a mustard seed. This was a tree I wanted moved, not a mountain, but the principle seemed the same. The thought entered my mind -- Jesus talked aloud to the Fig tree and His disciples heard Him. And that tree obeyed Jesus' command. I recalled a verse in Luke 17:6 that if we spoke to a Sycamore tree and told it to move, it would obey, if we didn't doubt. But believing what we said would come to pass was part of the condi-tion.

The next morning I looked the verse up and read it. It sure did apply to my need. But it was up to me to go out and speak to the tree! I thought about it all day at work. What would Bill say? Or the neighbors, if they saw me?

"That crazy neighbor is out there, talking to a tree!"

"Maybe I should wait till dark?" the thought crossed my mind. But after dinner, I went out while Bill was busy cutting grass, and hoped no one saw me. I really felt foolish.

"In the name of Jesus, tree, I command you to move. To move over enough to install this unit. Thank You, Father, for hearing my prayer and for Your promise that this tree has to move -- if I believe. I do believe it will happen and I thank You for it, in Jesus name." I went back in the house. I didn't measure the tree, nor its location; I just knew God would take care of it.

The installers came and worked most of the day. As they were preparing to leave, Bill called me to look at the new unit -- there it was, beside the tree! I was thrilled.

"Oh, you didn't have to cut the tree after all!" I exclaimed.

"No," Bill said, "they thought it was ok after all."

Then I told Bill what I had done and about talking to the tree. "You are kinda weird, honey, but the Bible does say that. Are you going to start talking to all the trees now?" He laughed and so did I, as I replied, "No."

But I did.

Three years later, we had our driveway lengthened and that same Dogwood tree was along the edge of the proposed new extension. Again Bill told me the tree would have to go. I just prayed about the tree and yielded the whole thing to the Lord. It was a beautiful tree but I was willing to have it removed. I didn't idolize the tree. Still, Jesus said if we spoke to it, it would move and I knew that was true. So I talked to that Dogwood again and told it to move over enough for the driveway, in Jesus name.

The work crew came and worked for hours, and at last Bill came to tell me it was finished. We went out to admire the 30 feet of parking space the shiny asphalt had created. There stood the tree -- with plenty of room to spare! Sunlight filtered through the leaves, making shadows on the new driveway.

"I'll probably trim back a couple of those limbs, so I can get the camper past without scratching it," Bill told me.

"Good idea, honey." I exclaimed. "I'm so glad they didn't have to cut the tree after all."

Seem a little far fetched? It was Jesus' idea, not mine. He said the tiniest mustard seed faith could do it and even move a mountain. I haven't had a mountain I needed to move -- yet. But if I ever do -- I'll be out there talking to it.

God honors His word and confirms it, when we act in faith trusting Him to bring it to pass.

Chapter 34

FAR FROM HOME WITH A BIG NEED

This testimony of God's provision should encourage you if you are stranded without money. Don't lose your confidence in God.

While Bill was away for two weeks hunting deer, I made plans to do something with my Mother. We decided to go to Germany to visit Lew, my oldest son, and his family.

We knew we'd be staying with Lew and Kay and wouldn't need much money, so we felt we could afford to go if we saved enough for our airfare. We also decided to go to London and return to the States from there. We wanted to sightsee and get down to South Chard and visit a Charismatic Church and some of the people whom we had met. We saved all year and thought we had planned adequately for a "budget" trip. We each had $400.00 plus our airline tickets when we said goodbye to Bill at Dulles Airport.

We were astonished in Germany to see how inflated their prices were and how our American dollar had been devalued. We enjoyed the German restaurants and food, but it made us really appreciate America. We realized Americans were spoiled by lots of food and cheap prices. We really took our land of plenty for granted. One man told us they loved to come to America because it was so cheap.

Lew and Kay took us sightseeing in Germany. It was just a thrill to see so many sights we'd only read about in history books. It was beautiful. The mountains, vineyards, quaint villages and huge old Cathedrals, we loved it all. But it wasn't so exciting to see our dollars dwindling away on bare necessities. "It was a good thing we didn't plan on buying souveniers!" I told Mom after a few days.

"We've got a surprise," Kay told us, "we're taking you to Paris for three days."

"We'd love it!" I said, "but I don't think we can afford it."

"Don't worry, Mom," Lew said, "We've saved our money and we're paying for our rooms. You can help with the gas and food." So off we went -- Thanksgiving Day -- driving to Paris!

It was even more interesting than I thought and much bigger. Lew and Kay spoke French and took us everywhere on the Metro. They

had been there before, so they knew just how to get to the Eiffel
Tower, Notre Dame Cathedral, and other famous places. The Arch de
Triumph had an "eternal flame" burning for a memorial to men who died
for their country. Beautiful flower wreaths were there. We were
told they were placed fresh daily by veterans groups.

There was so much to see and those darling grandchildren, Mary
Chris, 9, and Danny, 4, never seemed to get tired or cranky, even
when we went to the Louve Art Museum!

"You can't leave Paris without going to the Louve, Mom," Kay
told me. "After all, you're an artist and you'll appreciate it even
more than the rest of us."

"Yes, I really would like to see a few things in it," I replied.
"Like the statue of Venus de Milo and the paintings like the Mona
Lisa, but I know everyone is tired."

"We're fine, Mom," Lew said, "and we want you to see it." Off
we went. It was a glorious three hours just seeing art by the famous
old masters I had studied in school.

"Another treat," Kay told us, "we're going to Versailles and see
the Palace. You can't leave France without seeing that, too."

"You've really spoiled us already," I said.

"Yes, our beautiful room has a bath, and I know that is costing
you a small fortune! I wish you'd let us pay for it," Mom told Lew
and Kay.

"It's our treat," Lew replied with a smile.

The Versailles Palace was more opulent and splendid than I'd
ever imagined. The kings had poured the countries wealth into this
magnificent structure and grounds. It was vast and I was astounded
at the art work. Paintings were so gigantic they covered a whole
wall, perhaps 15 x 30 feet. The ceilings were paintings, too. It
was a delight to an art lover like me. I just couldn't rush through
our tour. History really came alive again and we had lots to talk
about on our return trip.

"I don't think I'll ever get over paying $2.00 for a "Big Mac,"
Mom said. It was a shock, when we stopped at a Paris McDonalds for a
treat from America.

The angels came to our rescue as we left Paris. Lew had a map,
but getting to the Autobahn wasn't shown and he needed help. Shortly
after leaving our hotel, he pulled over to the curb to study the map
a bit more. The traffic was heavy in this downtown area. Suddenly a
man leaned over and tapped on the window of Lew's little Toyota.
None of us saw him walk up to the car, so it startled us. He spoke
to us in German. Lew replied and they talked and pointed to the map
and down the street. Lew nodded and smiled.

"Merci, beaucoup," he told the man, and waved as Kay rolled the
car window back up. The man disappeared almost instantly in a crowd
crossing the street.

"It must have been an angel," I said. "He just came out of
nowhere and knew exactly what you wanted to know. And he could speak
so you could understand and then disappeared so quickly."

"We'd have never found this shortcut," Lew announced happily.
"It must have been a grey haired angel in a brown suit." We all
laughed over God's provision to meet our need. It was snowing as we

headed back to Germany. What a beautiful sight!

"We'll never forget our wonderful visit," Mother told Lew and Kay.

"You've spoiled us," I said. "It's been so wonderful being with you and the children. It makes it hard to leave and be so far apart." It was true. Lew had been stationed so far away from home in his 12 years with the Air Force, we just rarely got to be with them.

"England will be a let down after all we've seen and done with you," Mom said, as we made our tearful goodbyes.

Little did we know what lay ahead.

"We'll have to go home!" Mother declared as we waited through airport customs lines. "There's no way we can spend 4 1/2 days in London on the money we have left!" She was right, however, our "supersaver" tickets didn't allow any changes in our plans and it would cost us full fare to go home those few days early. It seemed we had no choice! We had to go on to London whether we had any money or not!

We counted our cash and traveller's checks and came up with $100.00 apiece. Mom and I had already planned to stay in an English home, if possible, and enjoy the less expensive bed and breakfast accommodations, mentioned in the "Europe on $15.00 a Day" book. I did some quick figuring and said, "I think we can manage, Mom, if we don't take any tours and have one big meal a day. But we'll have to get the least expensive rooms we can find. At any rate, we can't go home. I know God will supply our needs!"

Aboard the plane, flying to London, Mother did begin to worry and talk about us running out of money. It was understandable, but didn't help to worry and only made her more fearful.

"Mom, please, don't talk about it anymore. We musn't lose our confidence in the Lord. He knows our needs and how little money we have. We'll do our part to stretch our money and God will take care of us." I continued assuring her, "Don't worry, honey. God loves us and He's not going to let anything happen now! He has given us such a wonderful visit with Lew and Kay. God gave us good weather all this time, so we could get out and travel in Germany and France. Lew said that was a miracle for this time of year. God isn't going to let us down now."

At the airport hotel reservations desk, I inquired about bed and breakfast rooms. The girl at the desk said she could only help with the big hotels. I explained we couldn't afford that and asked about transportation into London. She was very friendly and helpful. She suggested the airport bus to Victoria, where the airlines had ticket offices. "There," she told me, "they can find you accommodations at the small bed and breakfast hotels. And it's the most convenient location for sightseeing. You can walk to the Palace and there are buses and trains right in the area." She advised us to cash our traveller's checks there as the exchange rates were better than in town.

We got the British Airways bus and headed into London. It was overcast and cool, but it seemed hot compared to Germany. Our bus arrived at the airline terminal and we went to the hotel reservations desk. The young lady told us they had lots of nice bed and breakfast hotels where two ladies would feel safe. She called and told us, "The cheapest rate is 12 pounds per night." It included breakfast, which was normally coffee or tea and roll.

We discovered at the airport bank, our dollar was about half the value of the British Pound. Quick calculations made it $24.00 a night, for four nights! That left us $100.00 for food, the bus back to the airport and everything else we'd need for the entire time for two people! It was scary to think about, so I refused to think about it. Instead, we rejoiced all the way to our hotel, as the rates downtown were more than double what ours was! The small hotel was like a row house but clean and pretty. Our room was off the main lobby, the only one on the first floor besides the owner's apartment. It was a large sunny room complete with table and chairs, and two twin beds, a sink and a mirror.

After resting for two hours, we decided to go out and find a restaurant before bedtime. It was raining now, but we were prepared. We found lots of nice places to eat and happily discovered menu and prices listed on each window. That helped! Meals were expensive compared to America. After dinner, we decided to walk to the Buckingham Palace, even though it was still raining and the street lights were dim. We inquired as to crime and safety of two women walking around alone at night.

"Oh, you are perfectly safe. We don't have the problems here you have in your country," the restaurant owner told us. It made us feel terrible that America had earned such a reputation, and even worse that it was true. Tourists couldn't be assured they were safe to walk about alone at night in our big cities.

We had studied our street map of London and found the Palace easily. We were amazed it wasn't lit up at night, like our White House, Capitol or other important buildings. Since we couldn't see much of the Palace, we decided to walk a few more blocks where the bright lights of Trafalgar Square were glowing even through the drizzling rain. As we began walking across the street from the Palace, we saw some buildings inside a high wall, with guards stationed at various places around it. It was a huge compound, but nothing on our map indicated what it might be.

"I wonder what building this is?" I asked aloud. "It must be important with the guards all around."

"Why don't you ask the man who is coming this way," Mom suggested. "I don't want to ask a stranger," I replied. But she urged me to do so, as he crossed the wet street coming toward us.

"Excuse me, Sir," I asked, "could you help us? We were wondering what this building is. It isn't marked in any way on our map and we know it must be important with all the guards around it. Could you tell us?"

"I certainly can!" He replied, "It is St. James Palace. It is a very important building. Much of the Royal staff and residences are here."

He looked at his watch. He was medium build, greying, a distinguished looking gentleman dressed in black. A pleasant smile broke out on his face as he looked up from his watch. "We're going out

126

tonight, but I have a few minutes," he said. "Would you like to come and see where the Guards assemble and the Queen's royal chapel?"

Of course we did! We followed him and scurried along the rain soaked street, as he chatted away about various points of interest around the area. Again, he glanced at his watch.

"Would you like to see the Queen?" he asked. "I know it's a dreadful night to be out."

"Oh, we'd love it!" We were both talking at once. We never dreamed we'd get to see the Queen while we were here! "We don't mind the rain."

"I think there's time, if you hurry along," he told us. "The Queen is going to attend "Hello Dolly" tonight, with your Carol Channing, at Drury Lane Theater." He proceeded to give us complete instructions, concerning which bus to take, where to get off and even where to stand near the theater.

"Stand right where I told you, and the Queen's car will come right alongside you. If you look closely, you'll see me," he told us. "I'm the Queen's chauffer." We were so astonished! How good the Lord was to let us see the Queen and meet some of the Royal staff.

"Are you ladies on a tour tomorrow?" he asked.

"No, we'll be sightseeing, but we haven't signed up for a tour," I replied. "We have our map and thought we'd walk and see the city."

"I won't be needed tomorrow," he said, "the Queen is having Investiture. I'd be happy to show you some places in the city, which most tourists never see."

My suspicious nature took over. "Oh, we couldn't do that," I replied. I wasn't about to meet a stranger for a tour around an unfamiliar city!

"We'd love it," Mother said. "Are you sure it wouldn't inconvenience you too much?"

I could hardly believe my ears! My cautious Mother was agreeing to meet a total stranger for a tour of London! I protested, but it did no good. These two people had hit it off and Mom felt perfectly safe. She was quickly planning a convenient meeting time and place for the next morning. I had visions of headlines blaring about "two American women slashed to death by Jack the Ripper." Maybe I'd read too many mysteries in my youth. Maybe my father's work in law enforcement, as a Deputy Marshal, had made me suspect the worst motives behind this friendly gesture. Nevertheless plans were set, all I could do was pray.

We said hurried "goodbyes" to Mr. "X" and started off for the nearby Drury Lane bus stop. The bus was coming! It only took 15 minutes to get to the spot where we'd been told to stand near the theater. Sure enough, "Hello Dolly" was listed. At least that much of what we had been told was true.

Flower baskets and a red carpet were stretched out near the curb and crowds were gathered across the street, watching the big cars and elegant people arrive and disappear inside the theater. It was raining hard now. We were really wet. The umbrellas only protected a portion of our body, but we were too excited to notice. A few people had come and joined us near the curb.

"When do you think the Queen will arrive," I asked a couple nearby.

"The Queen is never late," they replied. "She is to arrive at 8 o'clock and she will be prompt."

"Does she have a police escort coming ahead of her," I asked them.

"Oh my, no! She just travels about like a commoner, but everyone loves her. It's not like your country," they told us. Again I felt badly that America had such an ugly reputation.

"How do you ever know it's her?" I questioned. They were very patient with me. "You'll recognize her car, it's a maroon Mercedes. It has a tiny blue light on it," the man told us. He hardly finished speaking when he spotted the blue light. "Here she comes now!" he exclaimed.

The car pulled to the curb and slowly passed us. So close to us in fact, we could see the Queen's lovely complexion and hair. It surprised me she had beautiful auburn hair. It looked dark in photographs. She was so beautiful in person, dressed all in white and a white fur. Everyone applauded and cheered as she got out and waved. And quickly, she disappeared inside. It was over. The people began to drift away.

"That was so exciting! We never dreamed we'd get to see the Queen," I exclaimed to the couple nearby, who had been so helpful.

"We go to see the Queen as often as we can. We watch the papers and try to welcome her, or see her off, when she travels about. I guess you can tell we are Royalists," the man responded.

"Will you be in London very long?" the lady asked.

"Another four days. It's our first trip and we want to see everything," we told them.

"We hope you have better weather for the rest of your stay," they said to us and they walked away.

Mom and I headed back to the bus stop. It was still raining, quite hard, and we were soaked. We asked about buses to Victoria Station. The people who were waiting there said, "You'd do better if you went two blocks over, as more buses to Victoria pass there." So we walked to the new bus stop, chattering all the way about how good God was to us, in letting us see the Queen!

"Oh, Nita, look -- it's the lady we met at the Theater," Mom said to me, and pulled on my sleeve. I was looking at the bus pulling toward the curb. It was marked "Victoria." I turned around and there was the lady we met at the theater standing beside us. She had been so helpful to answer our questions regarding the Queen. What a surprise!

"We've been driving all around trying to find you," she said. "We started to go home and we both felt just terrible that we hadn't been more friendly and offered to take you to your hotel."

"Oh, my goodness," I replied, "we wouldn't expect that!"

"Do come along and let us give you a lift to your hotel," she said.

"We couldn't," I replied, "we really couldn't. I wouldn't get into anyone's car, as wet as I am! Thank you so much for offering. You are really so kind, but we'll just hop on a bus and get home."

"Well, I think we should take up their offer, Nita," Mother said. "These nice people have driven all around, trying to find us, and I think we should accept their offer." So we got into their little car which was waiting at the curb.

"Hullo," the man said as we climbed in. "We found you in all these crowds because we remembered your bright-colored umbrella. That's how we found you." It was the umbrella that Maidie had given me for my birthday. This was the first time I had needed it. I couldn't wait to tell her how God had used it. After asking where we were staying, they introduced themselves as Win and Ralph Martin. They lived in London and just loved the Royal family and were proud of their native land. It delighted them that we were so enthusiastic about their Queen and our visit.

"Could you let us make up for our being so thoughtless, and let us take you for a little drive around and show you the city?" Win asked. "It is lovely at night, even in the rain."

"Of course, we'd love it...but that is a lot for you folks to do," I replied, "and we don't want to impose. We're so grateful for a ride."

Well, these dear people were fabulous! They drove us all around town and across every bridge, and explained the history of points of interest all along the way. Stopping by the Houses of Parliament and letting us see the Tower of London and "Big Ben" and all the famous places, all lit up. It was beautiful! We chattered along the way, and expressed our delight to see so much of the city.

I guess we must have talked about the Lord, for they asked if we'd be interested in seeing the John Wesley Chapel near Aldersgate Street. We were overwhelmed. Since I had been a Methodist for 15 years I was really interested in the founder, John Wesley. I never thought I'd get to see the place where John Wesley had his "experience," which made the spiritual change in his life. But here we were seeing it, and having Christian people drive us around and explain everything along the way! God was so good!

"Do you ladies drink?" Ralph asked. When we said, "no," he quickly said, "we'd like to take you to a famous Pub called The Anchor. It is one that wasn't destroyed in the great London fire. It is famous because it used to be a prison and called The Clink. Many people never see it. It's out of the way, but it is a nice place. They serve meals and it's very proper. You ladies won't feel uncomfortable. We can get a cup of coffee or tea. What do you say?"

"Oh, we'd love it," I heard Mom say. I wasn't so sure. I was having those suspicious thoughts again. Why were these people being so nice? Were they out to rob us? They "appeared" to be such nice, middle-aged, polite people. But why were they going out of their way, so much, for two women who were total strangers? I suspected the worst!

Maybe they'd get us in some dark alley and rob us! Or kill us! Maybe we'd be used as hostages in some international spy plot. After all, I did work at the Pentagon. That probably would be useful to spies. All these thoughts crossed my mind, but I didn't know how to get them to just "take us to our hotel."

We drove down some very dark alleys and small places where only a tiny car could have driven. I was becoming more alarmed all the time. They could throw our bodies in a dark warehouse and no one would ever find us!

Oh, why had we accepted a ride from strangers? I was praying fervently.

"Here we are," Ralph said. "Sorry it's such a miserable night for your first visit to London." They ushered us into the Pub. It was interesting and I was happy to see there were quite a few patrons in the place, and some of them were women. There were dining tables and they guided us to a little room off to one side, where there was a nice fire in the nearby fireplace. They ordered coffee and tea.

As we sat talking, they explained about the old prison and how people who were brought here usually never left alive. The chains that held them were still hanging on the walls...neck and wrist and leg irons! Some were brought here for being poor debtors. The "Clink" didn't supply food for the prisoners. Either friends or family had to bring in food. If you starved or froze, that wasn't the concern of the keepers, surely different from the USA prisons today!

"We'd like to invite you ladies to come up to our flat, if it isn't too late," Win said. "We'd like for you to see how the British people live. It isn't fancy, but it is comfortable and convenient for our getting to work."

"Oh, that would be wonderful," Mom replied, "it isn't too late for me!"

Again...I was so suspicious, and I didn't want to go! I just wanted to get to the hotel, safely. I was beginning to think we were part of a "spy movie" and the plot was getting thicker. What was coming next?

But we were soon back in the car and driving to their flat. The streets were pretty deserted and dark in the rain. It was almost 11 p.m. when we pulled to a stop at the apartment. I had no idea where we were, just somewhere in London. I still hesitated to follow this couple into the building. It was late and only a few lights on anywhere in the surrounding area! The whole building looked deserted. Mother just followed along, talking happily with Win. Ralph walked briskly ahead of them.

I lagged behind. I was looking for any signs of "help" if we should need it.

"Let me take your coats, I'll just put them in the bathroom, if you don't mind. Make yourself at home," Ralph said cheerfully. "The news is just coming on if you'd like to see if there is any break-through in the hostage situation...isn't it dreadful?"

Their "flat" was just lovely, so modern and beautifully furnished, with a garden balcony and a nice view. They had a color TV and we settled down to watch the first news since we'd left the USA for our vacation. Nothing had changed much. Win came in with a lovely tea service and "biscuits," which we discovered were delicious cookies. They were just so wonderful to us, and I was grateful for the hospitality. After tea, Win took us around to look over the apartment, which was spacious and well equipped, including a freezer in the kitchen. Ralph was very proud of that new addition to their home. I'd heard of "bodies" being hacked up and hidden in a freezer! I just wanted to get to our hotel.

We were talking of leaving and Win asked Ralph if he would drive us to the hotel, as she wasn't feeling good. We learned that she was home convalescing from surgery. She worked for the Post Office, a Government employee -- just like me! Win had been more than gracious and generous with her time, to entertain strangers. We knew it had to be God's love being showered on us through Win and Ralph.

"Could we have prayer together before we leave?" I asked, and they said they'd be happy to and asked me to lead it. I did and got choked up, thinking of their kindness. I asked God to "really bless these dear people, who had befriended us." I prayed for Win's complete healing and for God to bless Ralph in his job, at the London power facilities. Win was crying when I finished praying.

They made us promise to call them before we left London, and to call them if we needed anything! It was midnight when we left their flat and headed across town to Victoria, and our hotel. Ralph assured us he didn't mind the drive and wouldn't think of letting us take a taxi. He managed to get us there quickly and waited till they unlocked the door for us, and waved a cheerful goodbye.

What a night! What a start for our visit of London!

We had seen the Queen! We had met her chauffer. We'd had a guided, driving tour of the entire city and had refreshments in a famous Pub. Then treated so wonderfully to tea in a British home. We hadn't spent any money except for dinner since we arrived at the hotel. When we finally crawled in bed, we were almost too excited to go to sleep!

What else could God have in store for us?

Chapter 35

JACK THE RIPPER

Breakfast at the hotel turned out to be a full meal! Ham, eggs any way you liked, toast and jelly and lots of coffee and juice. We were stuffed! Since we didn't know if we could afford lunch, we ate every bite! Then we hurried off to meet Mr. "X," the Queen's chauffer, for a guided tour of the city. And what a tour it was! He told us he had escorted many of our visiting dignitaries. "No one could keep up with me," he told us, "for it requires a lot of walking to see London properly."

We started off at the Buckingham Palace and among the shops, including the Royal Grocer, "Fortnum and Mason." He wanted us to go in and look around. I couldn't afford anything, but wanted to see it. I was astounded to see the clerks in Regal uniforms and carpet on the entire floor! I wanted to buy some sugar, Lew and Kay had told us about, which the British serve. It was colorful and a bit grainy, but quite elegant. I couldn't afford much, but decided to buy two pounds to take back for gifts to our family and friends. Later I regretted this purchase, as I carried that two pound load all over London for over eight hours!!

We covered the Art Gallery, Fleet Street, and St. Paul's Cathedral. Mr. "X" pointed out there was an "American Altar" there, in honor of the American military service men who defended London in World War II. Next we went to the Stock Exchange to watch the action. Then on to Mary Le Bow Church with its secret stairs and tunnels. Next we passed the open markets on Poultry Street and the London Museum where we saw a film of the 1667 fire. The museum contained part of the old Roman walls and the Lord Mayor's regal carriage. It was most interesting and often missed by tourists.

Next we saw the "Curiosity Shop," a tiny building mentioned in a Charles Dickens book, and the Pub across the street from Scotland Yard, where Arthur Conon Doyle wrote "Sherlock Holmes" stories. It was about 5 p.m. and my feet were aching. I said we were going to have to call it a day. Mr. "X" told us we couldn't skip the legal and judicial area, which was nearby and suggested we have some refreshments and rest a bit.

He had treated us to lunch, and now we stopped at the famous Cheshire Cheese Pub. It was crowded. Many people knew Him and chatted with him and greeted us. We were glad to sit down! We must have covered 20 miles or more! I was ready to head back to the hotel, and bed! I told him so.

"You must see the Temple area," he said, "it isn't far." And off we went.

He was taking us to a dimly lit area and fewer and fewer people were around. I felt uneasy. It was getting dark now.

It was interesting and I asked if it had anything to do with Freemasonry. He asked how I knew about that. I told him that my Uncle was a Mason. Later on, he pointed out several places of interest regarding Masons. Perhaps the most interesting was a cornerstone inscribed in the Temple building with leadership by the King of England.

It was after 6 p.m. now.

Mr. "X" said he knew the "perfect place" for us to have dinner. They served a delightful buffet of various English dishes, so we could sample that type of cooking. He liked to take visitors there and wanted us to enjoy it as well. I didn't want to go any further with this stranger.

"I can't eat a bite," I exclaimed. "I am too tired to eat! I just want to get a taxi and head to our hotel."

"How are you, Mum," he asked Mother.

"My Mother would agree to anything," I thought to myself. He had been pleasant all day, but I didn't like him "pushing."

It was almost dark.

"Well, I am fine," Mother said.

"It's been just wonderful," I told him, "but I've overdone it. We really must get a taxi and get back to the hotel and rest." I was determined to go nowhere else with this stranger. He laughed. His energy was amazing for he wasn't a young man.

"I've brought her to her knees," he said. I didn't like that expression! It made me suspicious. Was that his plan to get us too tired to think straight and get us to a secluded place? To rob, rape or kill us?

Who would miss us?

"I'll get a taxi for you," he said. Before we knew it, he was inside the cab and telling the driver where to go in Victoria. Again I got more suspicious! Would we have trouble getting rid of him? Would he try to force himself on us? We were pretty defenseless, all alone in this city. Who would know we were even missing? Only the hotel, and our room was paid for the balance of the week, so they probably wouldn't even care.

Again, I was praying for God's help and watchful care, as well as asking forgiveness, because we'd behaved foolishly in accepting this friendly hospitality.

"I want to send you a calendar from the Palace staff," he told us as we were leaving him.

"You've been so generous and have done so much for us now! How can we ever thank you?" I asked. My suspicions about Jack the Ripper were disspelled.

"We can truly say that we've seen London! And a guided tour by an expert! It was grand," Mother told him. We agreed to his one request, that we write him from America. And he was one on his way.

Two years later Mother was watching Prince Charles' wedding on TV and she recognized Mr. "X" driving a royal carriage. She was so excited to see him again.

What a day! What more could God do for us?

Our second day and we hadn't spent any money at all that day! God knew how to stretch it.

Chapter 36

THE LAST TRAIN

The next morning, at breakfast, we decided to take a train down to Chard, and look up the Charismatic Church and people there. We were too tired to walk anymore! Though we still wanted to see the inside of the Tower of London. That was the only thing we'd missed on our tour!

We went to Victoria train station and got a train almost immediately, heading to Chard. We didn't take any luggage as we planned to return that evening on the last train at 8 p.m. We would just have a nice visit and meet the people. So we thought. God had other plans for us. Another blessing.

The countryside was so interesting all along the trip. The quaint towns and buildings were like those we had seen only in history books, many older than America! After the train, we took a bus for an hour's ride to reach the little town of Chard.

"All I remember is Uncle Sid's last name, Purse. I do hope he's listed in the phone book," I said to Mom. Sure enough, there it was.

A friendly lady answered and I told her who I was, from the USA and that we'd come to visit them, if they wouldn't mind. "Oh, how wonderful, where are you now?" the friendly lady asked. "I'll send a car around for you in a few minutes."

Before we could buy some "goodies" at the bakery next door, a car arrived with three men...to carry our bags! We didn't have even one! They were so happy to see us and introduced themselves as we headed for the "Manor House." The quaint old building, the "Manor House," they told us, was over 400 years old. The thatched roof had to be redone about every five years in sections. They wanted us to see the church Uncle Sid had built with his own hands, and the new buildings, for housing and a fellowship hall. It was a regular complex to care for the hundreds of people who came for ministry from Europe and other countries.

"I'm Auntie Mill," the jolly heavy-set woman said, flinging her arms around us both. "Uncle Sid's upstairs, ministering to someone, but come right on in and have some tea." "Now, where are you from?

135

Where are your things? How long can you stay? Have you had dinner?
Come and meet the others," she made us feel right at home.

We met some delightful people who had come there for a holiday
and ministry as well. One couple was especially friendly to us.
Walter and Margery Pipe wanted to know all about where we were from
and where we'd been on our first trip to England. They all seemed so
surprised that we'd gotten to see the Queen on our first and very
brief visit.

Walter and Margery were like sweethearts, though they had been
married 32 years. "Jesus has given me a new husband," Margery told
us. Walter enthusiastically told us he had been saved recently and
baptized in the Holy Spirit just three weeks prior to our arrival.
"I am a new man," Walter said.

Soon it was time to eat and we learned there was to be a midweek meeting that very night. What a thrill! We never expected to
be there for a meeting, even though that was our heart's desire,
after hearing so many of the meetings recorded on tapes.

"Can't you stay for the meeting?" they asked us. Uncle Sid had
joined us by that time, for the evening meal.

"No, we only bought a ticket for one day, and we must take the 8
p.m. train back to London," I told them. "Unless there is a later
train or we could change our tickets for tomorrow."

We called and found there were no later trains and the tickets
were not good after the time indicated.

"I'll drive you to the train station myself, if you'll stay,"
Walter Pipe volunteered. "We will even drive you to London, if you
need us to, couldn't we, Margery?" he asked his attractive wife.

"Oh, we couldn't let you drive us to London, but the train
station would be great. We would like to stay," Mom and I both
chimed in.

"Well, it's settled then," Auntie Mill told us. "My nighties
will fit anyone and we have plenty of room. You might get a bit
cold, as we don't have central heat, but we have plenty of hot water
bottles so we'll fix you up."

Auntie Mill and Auntie Edith Haines fixed sandwiches and soup
and served the bakery "goodies" that we had brought. Mother and I
went into the kitchen as they prepared the meal. They told us that
they served lunch to everyone who attended the Sunday service! That
was 200 or more people to cook for. Those two women had a ministry
of serving and hospitality!

"I can't preach, but I can cook and that is how I support my
husband's ministry," Auntie Mill told us. "I've done it for many
years, to make beds and provide a place for people who come."

The evening meeting was in the fellowship hall and soon it was
crowded with people. Some remembered us and came to hug and welcome
us. They were surprised. We were too. And how good to renew
fellowship with Trevor and Sue Lancashire and Frank and Kathleen
Paine, and meet their daughter, Joy. How good to meet some of the
people we'd only heard of on tapes! We were delighted to meet Harry
Greenwood's wife, Pam, and especially their daughter, Jill, who
played the piano so beautifully! We'd heard of her, when she was

about 10 years old. We had learned a song the Lord had given her from Psalm 141.

What a meeting! What a night of praise and ministry! During the meeting the Lord gave me a vision which I shared. We were blessed. "I want to give an offering to the Lord," I told Mother, and took out Twenty Pounds in English money and gave it. Mom had her checkbook and wrote a check.

"Do you think we should give so much? You know we still have a lot of time to get by before we leave for home?" Mom reminded me.

"I have to show God how much I appreciate His wonderful care for us! I couldn't do less," I replied.

The next morning Auntie Mill fixed breakfast for us and Walter was up early and drove us over to catch the 8 a.m. train and buy new tickets. It cost us a lot but it was worth it! Mother and I were rejoicing that God had provided a way for us to miss the last train and have a wonderful evening with new friends. Walter said he wished he'd known we wanted to go to the Windsor Castle that day. "Margery and I would be happy to take you there, for we would enjoy going again, too," he said. But we wouldn't hear of it. Margery wasn't feeling very good and had stayed in bed that morning. The train came while we were having tea. We said our goodbyes and promised to write, never dreaming that a year later Margery would be near death. She wrote many times and her letters were so joyful and full of praise even when she was in terrible pain. The joy of the Lord was her strength.

As we headed for Windsor Castle and a day of sightseeing there, we planned to arrive in London with time for touring the Tower of London and seeing the famous jewels. I was sure they'd never let tourists see the prison, where so many "heretics" were kept for burning and beheading, but I wanted to see this famous place.

Meanwhile, touring the Castle at Windsor gave us the desire to pray for Queen Elizabeth and her family. We saw some beautiful hanging tapestries, which we had been told were Biblical scenes. They turned out to be only one from the Bible, the others were mythology! We have prayed for the Queen often since then. The grounds were lovely and everything historically interesting. We were glad we had seen it, but didn't think we would like to live in a big castle.

We arrived at the Tower of London half an hour before closing time...too late. No one was allowed in after that time. No exceptions. It was the only thing we'd missed on our tour of London! We headed to find a restaurant and have dinner.   We saw there was a performance of the "Messiah" at Westminister Abbey that evening and decided it would be a treat for our last night in London. After dinner we walked to the Abbey, which wasn't far. The performance was grand and the building was interesting, but not nearly so beautiful as St. Paul's Cathedral. Recently, we could understand why Prince Charles and Lady Diana had chosen St. Paul's for their wedding instead!

We had never really unpacked and we didn't have much to do the next day before plane time. It gave us time to write cards and catch the airport bus. We still had money left!

God had really blessed us two little ladies who had a big need, far from home with no money.

Chapter 37

GOD SUPPLIES, IN HIS TIME

God does supply our needs, not always as soon as we want, however. The waiting tests our trust in God.

Prayers helped a friend through a financial emergency. She drove to work with the gauge on empty. We prayed. That night heading home she asked God to help her get home and provide for her children. Traffic was heavy and slow -- burning up lots of gas sitting in bumper to bumper traffic. Thoughts of worry and fear flooded into her mind. She didn't even have money for a phone call if her car conked out. How would she get clear across Washington to her home?

No gas. No money. No food for dinner.

"Thank You, Lord, that Your Word says You will supply all my needs through Christ Jesus," she murmured praise and pushed the doubts from her mind.

God spoke to her, right there in the traffic! "Go home and take all the food you have in your house to Mrs. W. as soon as you get home."

"But Lord," she replied, "I don't have enough food for our own dinner and Mrs. W. lives back across Washington!! You know the car is running on fumes now."

"Gather all you have and take it to Mrs. W.'s house. You will be blessed," was God's response.

The children were puzzled to see their Mom going through the cupboards and freezer filling a bag with odds and ends of groceries. Instead of fixing dinner, my friend told them she would be back soon but she had to go and see Mrs. W. She was a friend, a widow, who was sick, and lived across town.

"Do your homework and pray for me, children. I don't have any money, no gas and no food for our dinner, but God said 'go' and I'm going. He's going to bless us. I know it." Off she went. It was almost dark when her car pulled up at the widow's address. My friend got out of the car and leaned in to get the grocery bag.

"Look down at your feet," God told her. She did -- it was still muddy from the rain and fallen leaves -- she didn't see anything.

"Look at your feet," the words came again.

All she saw was the muddy mess of leaves, but she bent down and picked up the little clump near her feet. She rubbed her hand over it and wiped some mud off -- it was money! Not leaves. But money covered with mud. She stuck it in her pocket, grabbed the groceries and went in to see Mrs. W. She was so glad she could encourage her and help her, even though the visit was short. Queen assured this lonely little widow that God loved and cared for her and had sent her there to tell her. They prayed together and promising she'd be back soon to visit, off she went, heading home.

Her first stop was the nearest gas station. She didn't even know how much money she had found. She took out the wet, muddy clump and saw there was a $10 bill on top. She filled up the tank. Joy flooded her, "Thank You, Jesus." Next stop, the grocery store, and she bought items for dinner and breakfast and lunches. She couldn't wait to get home.

"Come in the kitchen children," my friend announced when she arrived, "and see what God has done." What a happy time -- as she related what happened and how God had provided for them, when she was willing to give what she had to help someone else.

"God's ways aren't our ways," she told them, "I had to go clear across town to get my blessing from God, it wasn't at our house. I wouldn't have it if I hadn't obeyed God."

She counted out the soggy bills -- over $300! Enough to pay the rent and more besides. Truly God could do exceedingly abundantly above all you could ask or even think.

At the Pentagon Ladies' Bible Class the next day, there was great rejoicing over the miracle of answered prayer and providing for this need in God's creative manner.

* * * *

Another need was supplied, but of a very different sort. Bea Werner had been raised by her Grandmother and loved her so much that it was causing her great agony to see her sick. She'd had different doctors and been in and out of hospitals, but was no better. Bea asked for prayer and would gladly have taken the illness herself if she could get her Grandmother well again.

"Is your Grandmother saved?" I asked Bea.

"I think so, she's gone to church and taken me all my life," Bea replied.

"Wouldn't it be terrible if she missed heaven, just because you didn't make sure?" I asked.

"Oh, I'd never forgive myself! Nita would you talk to her? You'd know just what to say and I'm not sure I would be able to," Bea responded.

"I'll be glad to," I told her. But her Grandmother worsened and was placed in intensive care. No one could see her but family, for brief periods. A day or two went by and Bea called me. "Nita, please come to the hospital at noon with me. I'm so afraid my

140

Grandmother won't live much longer and I've just got to be sure she's Born Again."

"How will I get in?" I asked. Well, she didn't know, but thought she might talk to the doctor or head nurse for a special "exception" for a few minutes. I went to the hospital with Bea and her husband, John -- I prayed all the way and God answered! They agreed to let Bea and I go in together, since I told them I didn't know her. She needed to know I was a friend and had come at Bea's request.

Poor woman. If she wasn't sick, she'd get sick just looking at all the gear monitoring her. She appeared to be asleep, but responded to Bea's calling her name. How she loved that grand-daughter of hers was apparent immediately for she beamed a happy smile, as if she felt fine! Our introduction was brief for we only had five minutes. I didn't waste a minute but got right to the important question of "where she'd spend eternity?" and Bea's concern about it.

"Oh, my dear, I accepted Jesus as my saviour when I was 17. He has been looking after me all these years. Yes, I know I'm going to be with Him, that was settled long ago," she told me. What music that was to our ears! To hear that confession of faith from her own lips was an answer to prayer! The balance of our visiting time was full of talk about Jesus and how we all loved Him!

It wasn't too long afterwards that the Lord did take Grannie home to be with Him. But now Bea was prepared for that loss, knowing they would be together some day. There would be no more pain, no more sorrow, and no more tears in heaven, but there was still some sorrow here. She missed her Grandmother.

Perhaps this doesn't sound miraculous, but we knew it was! There was no way I could have gotten permission to enter that hospital room. I wasn't a family member. I wasn't clergy. I had no reason to be there, except God made a way. And not only for me, but for both of us to be allowed to go in at one time, when even the family had not been given that privilege. We knew it was God's way of answering the cry of Bea's heart and letting us be sure of her salvation! PTL!

* * * *

Tilly Fowler experienced a small miracle recently when her family heard an explosion outside their mobile home! They looked out and saw water gushing from underneath their home. It was dark and their flashlight wouldn't work. Tilly was frantic! She prayed a quick prayer for God to fix that flashlight and help Joe find the problem. Guess what? The flashlight worked perfectly when she pushed the switch! And Joe had the same results. Outside, he was searching for the source of the water cut-off, without success. He also prayed for God to help and God didn't let him down. He found the right valve! They both prayed about the repair costs and when the serviceman handed them the bill, they could hardly believe it. Only $3.00 for a new part. Isn't the Lord good? He can supply our needs instantly when the situation is urgent, or He can make us wait.

141

We must trust that "all things are working out for our good" because God loves us.

Ask our loving heavenly Father for big things, as well as little things. We have a big God...who is able to do much more, no, exceedingly, abundantly above all that you could ask.

What is the biggest, most impossible thing you can think of...something you need right now? Something that seems it could never happen. Well, God can do more than that!! He is bigger than any of our problems. He is bigger than any of our needs, and He loves you. He really does!

When no one cares for you...God does!

When no one can help you...God can!

When there is no one to talk to about your problem...God hears!

When no one knows your pain and suffering...God does, and He cares.

When others turn away from you...God never does.

He will never leave you.

God loves you. He really does.

Get a neighbor or a friend and just set aside a time each day to pray together, and start to see miracles in your own life.

There are conditions, however, and hinderances which might prevent God from answering your prayers. I want to share that with you as well.

Chapter 38

GOD DIDN'T ANSWER EVERY PRAYER

Before you groan and say, "it was because we lacked faith," or didn't pray "believing prayers," let me assure you that God can't answer some prayers.

But some will argue that "God can do anything"...and He can!

But he won't do some things, because it would go against His Word. He has said His Word is settled in heaven. It will never change. We can depend on it, and depend on Him to perform what He has said. Praise God!

Let me give instances of seemingly unanswered prayer.

There was a man working in the Pentagon who was terribly crippled. We'd seen a lot of handicapped people and always admired them for their efforts to be productive workers. We were glad the government hired disabled veterans and others who had similar limitations. This man was able to get around with two crutches, but with much difficulty. Everyone really pitied the man and we had prayed for him at various times.

One morning a young Naval officer came into the prayer group and brought the crippled man with him. He asked that we'd pray for him to be healed. It was exciting...we knew God could do it! No one had ever thought to invite the man to come to the meeting and be prayed for. Everyone gathered around and we prayed. After prayer we expected him to jump up and be able to walk normally. He didn't. We encouraged him that God sometimes healed instantly and sometimes it took awhile, but he would get better. He thanked us and left, with as much difficulty as when he'd arrived. But then, everyone had to leave for their offices and we scurried out of the Meditation Room.

Weeks passed and I kept seeing the man. He was still as crippled as ever. It always hurt my heart so much. I couldn't understand why God hadn't done a miracle for him, just as He had done for others. I prayed about it and asked God, "Why?" The reply was quick in coming. "He doesn't want to be healed," God spoke to me!

I could hardly believe it. Who wouldn't want to be normal? Who wouldn't want to be off those crutches and able to walk and be like

143

everyone else? That very day I met the man, and I stopped to talk with him. He always seemed happy to see me. After we had chatted a few minutes, I asked him how he was doing.

He said, "About the same."

"Have you been crippled very long?" I asked him.

"Since I was a young boy," he replied.

"Would you like to be able to walk normally," I continued, "and never have to use those crutches again?"

"Well, I'm not sure," he said. "You see," he told me, "I have a special place to park now, right next to the building. And I'd have to give that up."

I could hardly believe my ears! There were some advantages to being disabled, at least in his own mind. "I'm used to it now, and I guess I don't mind these crutches," he concluded.

I went away sorrowful, and yet I knew that God wouldn't do more than this man wanted. If he wanted to be disabled, God would allow it, though He had heard our prayers for his healing. God wouldn't override the man's own desires.

* * * *

Another instance I recall vividly though it was completely different.

A woman attended our prayer group and Bible studies and God had answered many prayers for her family and other needs she'd expressed. She knew God could do anything we asked. One day she came to class and announced that she was scheduled for surgery, "but I don't want you to pray for a miraculous healing."

"I don't want God to heal me," she told us, "I have Blue Cross and they will pay for everything. I will be home for six weeks convalescing." She continued, "I need some time off and I want to have this surgery."

She had the surgery as planned.

The next day I had a call from her hospital bed. "Please pray for me," she said, "I'm in so much pain, I can't even pray for myself." We did pray.

The Ladies' Bible Class sent flowers and several went to see her. The surgery wasn't successful. Somehow the bones didn't do what they were supposed to do and she would have to undergo more surgery.

She wanted prayer now, and she needed it.

Weeks and months went by. There were three operations and still the pain was constant. She finally decided to retire on disability. We tried to convince her that this was a poor confession to God's healing power, to say you couldn't work any longer. But again, she wanted to have some time off to do what she wanted and enjoy her home. Even after staying at home for over a year, she was still unable to do anything without pain.

The Bible says you get what you say. She said she was disabled, and she was. She didn't enjoy her retirement. She had more surgery and problems. We had prayed for her healing. Prayers of faith. But God wouldn't over-ride this woman's own desires.

As to why God didn't answer some prayers for some people, and He did for us...I really can't say. I just know He can!

Nor can I tell why God didn't heal some people...I just know He can!

God has reasons for not answering every prayer. Usually it is for our good. We just have to remember God loves us, but sometimes He can't give us what we want. He won't give us a bike before we can walk or talk. Sometimes maturity is involved. Sometimes He has to correct us. At least that was what happened to me. My own testimony is painful to relate, but maybe it will help you. That is my motive and my prayer as I write it.

I asked for prayer one early morning at the Pentagon for a sore throat. I had noticed it the night before as we drove home from prayer meeting. The Lord had given me wonderful health, and I wanted to keep it.

My throat got worse and I developed a cough. It wasn't too serious, but although I was praying and others were as well, the cough grew worse. I began to get embarrassed. I had given my testimony of God's healing me and giving me wonderful health, and now I sounded like I had tuberculosis!

I began to ask God "why" this had come on me, but nothing came to my mind. I asked the elders of the Church to pray and anoint me with oil and they did. Still I continued to get worse! I was coughing up phlegm in large clots, and my chest hurt. I knew it was serious and I should see a doctor, but I also knew that God could heal me. "Maybe I just need someone to pray a prayer of faith over me," I thought. So I called my friends, Major Myrl Allinder and Colonel Jerry Curry and asked if they could come to the Meditation Room and pray for me. I was desperate, and they said they'd be there at noon. I expected them to come and lay hands on me and pray mighty prayers of faith and the Lord would instantly heal me. I'd seen it happen before.

"What were you doing when you noticed the sore throat the first time, Nita?" Myrl asked. I searched my mind and remembered leaving the home prayer meeting, and Dill remarking that I must have sat too near the open window and gotten chilled. I remembered that I did get cold. Yes! That was probably the reason. I told Myrl that was what had occurred.

"Do you remember what happened just before you went home? Did anything happen that was unusual that night?" Myrl continued to ask me questions instead of praying for me.

"No," I replied, "nothing I can think of." But deep inside me, there was something that had come to my mind. I didn't want to think about it. "Have you asked the elders of your church to anoint you and pray for you?" Jerry Curry asked. I told him I had done that. "Then we'll just pray and agree with them for God's healing of this condition," Jerry said. Then both men prayed and laid their hands on my head.

"I feel better!" I told them, and I did. The pain in my chest was gone and I could breathe much easier, without the wheezing I had before. I returned to my office "happy as a Lark" -- singing the chorus "God is so good." He could do miracles -- and He had! It was

145

the best I'd felt in a month.

I didn't cough anymore. What a relief!

About an hour later, I had another coughing spell, as bad, or worse, than before. Someone in the office said, "You should get to a doctor." I agreed, but managed to finish out the day. I knew God had shown His healing power and answered the prayer of faith Myrl and Jerry had prayed. But something was preventing me from being healed. I knew I had to get serious with God.

I began to think of all the things that had occurred at the prayer meeting, the night I got sick. It was a wonderful meeting! We had a big crowd of Midshipmen attend. It was almost graduation and there were many testimonies about God's help in final exams. The singing and praise were jubilant, even more so than usual.

During a period of praise, the Lord gave me a vision. It was exciting for me, to have God give me anything, and this Word of Knowledge was a beautiful gift of the Spirit I knew I should share. Normally, if anyone had a vision, there was prayer afterward for the interpretation and then that was shared. Often prophecy followed, relating to the vision, or the Bible study for the evening would be relevant to it. It was always uplifting and encouraging when this gift of the Spirit was given. I was given several visions in the past, and I was always excited about it. It was like a dream -- only you were wide awake, and you would just see what ever it was -- as if it were on a movie screen.

That night I saw something "odd," I didn't know what it was. It was dark all around and I saw this small, odd-shaped thing falling down slowly in front of me. Then there was another of these objects that fell down and it joined close by the first one. There was another and another floating down and joining together with each other. Although they were similar, they were all slightly different. I wondered what in the world it could be!

More of these objects were fluttering together and joining the rest. Then I realized what it was. It was a flower! Like a Rose, with many petals. It was a beautiful flower. I prayed and asked the Lord what this vision meant, and quickly the words came to my mind. We believers were like these petals. Each petal was slightly different, but beautiful and fragrant all by itself. But when we came together, we formed something really beautiful. Something that we could never be by ourselves. God loved us each singly, but found great pleasure when we joined ourselves and came together. PTL!

I was thrilled! I shared my vision as soon as the song was ended. I expected them to rejoice, as I had, over this Word from the Lord to us, by the Spirit. Instead a Midshipman started singing a song! And one song followed another till our Bible study began, and almost before I knew it the meeting was over! No one had paid any attention to my vision, it was almost as if I didn't even share it!

I was hurt. Why hadn't they prayed over it? Why didn't they praise the Lord for this beautiful revelation? I resented it!

My throat felt sore, as I left the meeting, "I guess I sat too close to the window," I thought to myself. Going home, Bill agreed the Elders should have taken "time out" to pray about my vision and not let the singing go on, as if I hadn't shared it. But he advised

146

me to forget about it. "After all," he said, "you told everyone, that was all you were supposed to do."

The next week, a Jewish believer attended the prayer meeting, and during the meeting, he had a vision, which he shared. Everyone rejoiced over it, and it was very encouraging, but I was hurt all over again! The thoughts of "how they hadn't appreciated my vision" flooded into my mind. Resentment and self pity did too.

"They missed the blessing," Hazel told me, "not you. God blessed you and wanted to bless them by the vision. You can't help what the response was to it. You shared it and that was what God wanted." She advised me not to "hold hard feelings." So I forgot about it. I buried it so deep inside me, I didn't think about it any more. But I didn't forgive them.

As the Holy Spirit had brought all this to my mind, I repented and asked the Lord to forgive me. And I forgave them. How stupid I felt for not having done that sooner. It was such a little thing.

The next morning my cough was worse! I stayed in bed. It gave me lots of time to think. I asked the Lord to show me anything that was preventing me from getting well. Into my mind popped another incident that had occurred months before. It was so minor, but I hadn't forgiven it. There it was, vividly lodged down inside me.

Bill and I had gone to an all day Air Show and we really enjoyed the morning, walking around and inspecting all the airplanes, displays and watching some parachute drops and demonstrations. The big flying events were scheduled in the afternoon and by then I was getting tired. There were seats available in the grandstand, but it was an additional expense and Bill felt we had spent enough on admissions, etc. "We can see just as well, standing here," he said...and he was right. Hundreds of other people were doing that as well, but my feet hurt, and I felt neglected. The Air Show was exciting and two hours flew past. But self pity and resentment kept me from enjoying the show or my husband very much. I complained of exhaustion going home and Bill apologized for not getting us seats, but it was too late. I felt unappreciated and resented his spending money on anything unnecessarily -- recalling how he wouldn't spend money on me. I buried that too, somewhere deep inside me, but I didn't forgive Bill.

As I lay there remembering these things I cried over my rotten attitude, and couldn't wait for him to come home so I could apologize.

"Honey," I said, "I need to ask your forgiveness for something." I told him of the incident and how he had hurt me, and I asked him to forgive my bitterness over such a little thing. He could barely remember it happening, but he forgave me. And I forgave him, at last.

I was sure I'd get well with all that bitterness out of me, but the cough lingered on several days more.

"Honey," I told Bill, "I think I should ask the Elders to forgive me and confess the resentment and unforgiveness I've had over the prayer meeting incident."

"Oh, I don't think God would expect you to do that," he said, "if you have forgiven them, that should be enough."

"Well, the Bible says 'confess your faults -- that you may be healed' and I want to be healed!" I concluded, "if I'm still coughing on Wednesday night, I'm going to confess it and ask their forgiveness at the meeting." However, I was sure hoping I wouldn't have to!

I got better! I wasn't coughing hardly at all, and I didn't have the pain in my chest anymore. Praise God! Wednesday night arrived, and the meeting was going great. Maybe I sang too much, but I started coughing. Hard. I couldn't stop. I got a drink, but it didn't help. I knew God wanted me to confess my sin.

I did. It was prayer time and the Elders asked if anyone needed prayer. I went forward and sat in the chair and asked for anointing for healing. "But first, I have a confession to make," I told them, "and I want to ask your forgiveness." I poured out all the rotten mess. There wasn't a dry eye. The Elders asked my forgiveness, too, for not being spiritually sensitive during the meeting, and missing a blessing God had for us all. God did a real healing that night, when they laid hands on me and prayed.

I didn't cough again. I was completely well from that night forward. I learned a hard lesson! The need for instant forgiveness was vital. It was not optional. Jesus said if we wouldn't forgive, then He wouldn't forgive us. It was as simple as that. God had to teach me this lesson.

God didn't answer every prayer. The prayers for my healing were full of faith, but God used the unanswered prayer to teach me something vital. He loved me enough to wait, even though He wanted me well.

Maybe every sickness doesn't have a "reason," but it's good to ask God if there is something standing in the way. Something that might be hindering the answer to prayer, such as some of God's conditions, which we will look at next.

Chapter 39

MEETING HIS CONDITIONS

There are some reasons why prayers aren't answered. Usually it's because the Bible has conditions, right alongside the promises, and people don't meet the conditions. It's that simple.

Reread the promises in the Bible and make sure you understand the conditions for getting them into your own life. Then pray and ask God if there is anything that is hindering your prayers from being answered, to show you what it is. He will.

One of the biggest hinderances to unanswered prayer is unconfessed sin and sin that we condone. We enjoy it! It doesn't seem too serious and we justify it because we see other people doing so much worse. But the Bible says, "If I regard iniquity in my heart the Lord will not hear me," Psalms 66:18. We must sincerely hate sin and turn from it, or God can't answer our prayers.

Perhaps you've had people ask you to pray for them, saying something like this, "I know I'm not where I ought to be, but pray for me," or "I'm just an old sinner but pray for me and maybe God will have mercy on me." It won't work! They don't have any intentions of giving up their adultery, their cursing, their drinking, or their cigarettes, yet they think maybe God will answer that prayer. Isaiah 59:2 says that "your sins separate you from God and He will not hear." God cannot go back on His Word. The only change will come from repentance.

Another reason for unanswered prayer is harboring unforgiveness, holding onto grudges. You know it is wrong but you stay mad and resentful. Matthew 6:14-15 tells us that your prayer answering is over, unless you forgive.

Close on the heels of this is getting relationships "right" by seeking to be reconciled. If anyone has "ought" against you, Matthew 5:23 says you are to go to them. Maybe you don't know what is wrong, they are just acting cold toward you. Go to them, seek their forgiveness for anything you've said or done. Or maybe someone has injured and hurt you, maybe they owe you an apology. But God says you go to them and seek peace, not once but forgive seventy times seven! In Matthew 18:15, 21-35, Jesus told about the importance of forgiveness. It isn't optional.

Other prayers are unanswered because of wrong motives. Prayer is serious business and we must analyze our prayers for selfish content, or we ask amiss.

Ask. Maybe we don't ask at all. Sometimes you hear of Christians who didn't pray and ask for what they wanted because they didn't think God wanted to do nice things for them. Just the bare necessities was all He wanted them to have. I think of our own love for our children and how we enjoy taking them to a circus or something to make them happy. Not that they need it, but just because we enjoy making them happy! God loves us just like that! We're His kids! And God says ask!

Another hinderance to prayer is lack of faith. Some Christians pray but have little expectation that God will really answer, or little confidence that God is a miracle working God. Little wonder that those prayers aren't answered.

Another hinderance is lack of patience, being unwilling to wait for the answer. Occassionally God will withhold the answer to see if we really want what we have prayed for or He may wait just to teach the lesson of patience. Abraham is a good example of patience mixed with faith. It took years. Then God answered.

Strife in the home ruins prayer life as we see in 1 Peter 3:6. God views the couple as one flesh and He expects them to think, act and pray together. When there is bickering and disagreement the answers to prayer are few. God wants harmony.

Another common hinderance is not giving God our time for prayer. The Christian world is full of believers who give their time and energy to all types of pursuits and pleasures and there is little time left for prayer or for God. Yet God's Word says that if we want all things to be added unto us, we must put Him first in our life, not last.

Some of the hinderances mentioned are definately sinful and in order to have your prayers answered you will have to determine that nothing will be overlooked, but everything sinful confessed and turned away from. God will forgive and cleanse you when you do and the "hot line to heaven" will be open again.

We don't want anyone reading this book to miss out on the joys of answered prayers and receiving God's blessings. I know there are Christians who say they have never had a prayer answered! If you listen to their prayers attentively, you might find they don't meet one vital condition. One that turns on the power of Heaven, and that is praying in the name of Jesus. They pray their whole prayer to the Father, and end the prayer "in Your name" or something similar, and never mention the mighty name, the name which is above every name, the name of Jesus. It is a condition for getting your prayers answered. It is repeated so many times in the New Testament it would fill a page to list the references. Jesus said, "if you ask anything, in my name, it will be done for you of my Father in heaven." Over and over again, we are told to ask in Jesus' name. Yet many, many prayers are offered up and His name is never uttered. Little wonder that God doesn't answer. It is like praying for the lights to be turned on in your room. You can pray all you want but if you don't turn on the light switch, you won't get any light. And so it is with prayers that aren't prayed in the mighty name of Jesus. No results.

The last hinderance is the biggest tragedy of all, and that is being a faithful church member and not being born again. You think you are a good Christian and you are heading straight to hell, maybe with a choir robe on! Maybe you've been brought up in your church. Even before you could walk your parents carried you to church and Sunday School, so you feel secure. You are outwardly so good and decent, and you give time and money to your church, so you must be a Christian, right?

Wrong!

That is one of the most deceptive things that there is. Sitting in a church for 20 years won't make you a Christian any more than sitting in a garage will make you a car! God has conditions, and He won't force anyone to meet them. Still He stands at the door of your heart, knocking, wanting to come into your life and bless you...if you will let Him come in.

Dear reader, won't you let Him in? He loves you! He really does.

There isn't anything you've said or done that is "too bad" for Jesus to forgive. If you were the only person in the world, no matter how rotten you may have been, God would still have sent His Son, Jesus to die...just for you.

God loves you! He really does.

If the Bible is true, and it is, then we must all stand before God and the Book of Life will be opened and only those who have acknowledged Jesus Christ as their Lord and Saviour will be written therein. Anyone not found with their names written in that book will be cast into a lake of fire, where there will be eternal torment.

Would a loving God do that? He says He will. We've got the "rule book." It's up to us to read it and play by the rules. In most games there is a "time out," where the team can talk things over. Would you like a time out about now? Would you like to stop just now and pray and talk things over with God?

He's waiting to hear from you...He's waited all your life. He loves you!

Just talk to God as you would your best friend. Ask Him to forgive you for all the rotten things you've done, the secret things no one even knows you did, except you.

Ask Him to forgive you for living this long without accepting His gift of eternal life and forgiveness of your sins, which is only possible through faith in Jesus and what He has done on the cross.

Tell Him that you believe Jesus is His only begotten Son, that He died on the cross and rose again just as the Bible says and that He is coming back again as God has said.

Ask Him to come into your life and make you the person He wants you to be.

Ask Him for friends to help you learn His ways and for a good Bible believing church. Then thank Him for saving you. For now, you are a "new creature" and everything will become new in your life.

You are born again by faith in Jesus and in the Word of God. Now tell people of your decision. It's absolutely necessary for you to confess this decision boldly. It's a requirement God has laid down. Read Romans 10:9-10.

God is a rewarder of those who diligently seek Him. That is His promise and He never fails to keep a promise. So be diligent and give God the first part of your day, not just a few crumbs of your time before you fall asleep at night. Being diligent requires good habits, and they are easier kept than irregular ones. Just be determined and get up early each day. Don't even think about it. Just put your feet on the floor when your alarm rings early, get up and wash up. Open your Bible and begin to put God first in your life and first in your day. It isn't impossible, but it isn't easy, and there aren't any shortcuts. God rewards those who diligently seek Him.

Start praying today. Expect a miracle a day, even if God has never answered a single prayer for you, ever. That will make it more exciting. Now that you are part of God's family...He wants to give you the desires of your heart! How do you think you will feel when you pray for someone with cancer and they get well? Or find someone you prayed for had an "impossible" need met? Just because you prayed? Life will never be boring. The blessings will roll in like ocean waves.

You can make a difference in your family, in your job, in your world, if you will meet God's conditions and if you will begin to pray.

Chapter 40

FOR SUCH A TIME AS THIS

Can you make a difference in the world? Can I make a difference in America? We've already seen what God can do when a few women pray, but what can we do when our whole nation seems berserk with filth, pornography and violence? Can a few people bring about a change on a national level? Can a few redeem many, as in Jeremiah 5:1?

The answer seems logical to many Christians, for James 5:16 says the "effectual fervent prayer of a righteous man availeth much." The fervent prayers of the men and women of God will avail much. It can bring about change in America. But the Bible says fervent prayer, not a lukewarm prayer, not a memorized prayer nor one read from a Church bulletin. When you think someone you love is dying, you pray fervently for their recovery. No lukewarm prayer will do. America is sick and everything moral and decent is dying all around us, yet many are praying lukewarm prayers. I'm afraid our Pentagon ladies group was in the same condition.

We prayed for ourselves and our personal needs, and seemed to take our freedom for granted. We seemed to take justice in our courts for granted and seldom thought to pray for our Judges, or lawmakers. We seemed unaware of what was happening to America, when our leaders were found to be open to bribery and other moral weaknesses.

We knew, from the Bible, that the ruler of a nation has more effect than any single person or group to bring about blessing or evil upon the people. Yet we prayed more fervently for our own personal needs than for our leaders.

Until one day in 1974, we received a letter from Maidie. In it she told of a vision that had been given at a prayer meeting she attended in South Carolina. It was of the Lincoln Memorial in Washington, D.C. and inside, the statue of President Lincoln was no longer in his erect position, but slumped over in sleep! Instead of gazing over the Capitol building and the city, the statue's eyes were closed in slumber. The words of the Lord came forth in the vision, that this represented the Christians in America, and in the nation's capitol. They had been lulled into slumber! The Christians were no longer alert and praying for the leaders, but had taken it for granted that the blessings of God would continue to be shed upon "America the beautiful." The vile and corruption and violence had come in and there was no intercessor to stand in the gap and plead with God for our nation.

The call to prayer was urgent in this vision, and the hearts of the ladies in the Pentagon Bible Classes were stirred to be intercessors for America. We confessed that we had grown cold and forgetful of prayer for our leaders and we determined to pray daily for America. We vowed to pray for our leaders, that God would raise up godly men, who would seek His ways to determine our national decisions and laws. This vow included the agreement to fast each Friday, as well.

Since that time we have kept our vow to fast and pray for our leaders, but it is easy to forget! It is easy to be too busy! It is easy to concentrate on personal needs and neglect fervent prayer for our nation and its leaders. We have to be careful, and take heed that we do not neglect the very thing we have been called to do, and that is to pray.

"Lift up the spirit of Esther," Lieutenant General Shaefer's wife, Caroline, told us, "that gentle and quiet spirit of Esther saved a whole nation. Seek this spirit, this same spirit for yourselves. You should realize that you have been put here for such a time as this. It is your prayers and your willingness to yield to God's way, and to pray for His will to be done in our land. To stand for truth and right and justice. That is what God wants and is precisely why He has placed you here in this building."

We have heard, from so many sources, these very words repeated over and over! How exciting to know that we did not get here by accident. God Himself has brought us here to the Pentagon to be prayer warriors, to be women of prayer who would support our nation.

It reminded me of the gigantic pillars in the Pentagon. They support so much weight. The building wouldn't stand long without these pillars. Yet, they are unnoticed, passed by without a thought. How much like those pillars are the Christians in the Pentagon! These praying women, unnoticed, and yet important like the **Pillars of the Pentagon.**

From Pennsylvania, Major General Jerry Curry's mother came to visit the Pentagon ladies group. "Mom" Curry spoke and her words rang with authority. Just as the prophets of old had spoken telling people of God's purpose and plan for them, she came to tell us of God's plan and purpose for us. "Let's turn to Isaiah 59:16 quickly now," she told us. "He saw there was no man and wondered that there was no intercessor, that there was no one to intervene. He's talking about God the Father. No one to intervene on behalf of truth and right."

"Do you see why the Lord brought you into the Kingdom, for such a time as this? That you are the intercessors? You could be classed the 'front line troops.' We're in a spiritual battle, you know that, and where you are working -- you are living right on the 'cutting

154

edge.'" Mom laughed at this point and continued, "right where things are happening in this world, in the spiritual battle that is taking place. That's right!"

"And you are the intercessors!" Mom told us, "You are the ones that stand between a Holy God and sinful men all around you, and the principalities and powers of wickedness all around you. Hallelujah! God is using you to stand for what is right, to stand for godliness and truth."

Mom Curry looked back to the Scriptures and said, "It says here, God looked in those days and He saw that there was no man to do that. In this day He has you! Oh glory, Hallelujah!"

"Paul tells us that we must put on the 'armor of God,' the armor of a heavy-armed soldier, which God supplies, that you may be able to stand up against all the strategies and deceits of the devil." Mom went on, "and you know how subtly he works, isn't that right? Even in those things that seem to be good, and seem to be right, even saints can get off into these things."

"Paul cautions us not to be 'children any longer, tossed by every wind of doctrine, and the cunning craftiness whereby men deceive' and we must be established in our faith," Mom told us, "we must know who we are. We know God is our Father, Jesus is our Lord and Saviour and the Spirit of the living God is living in us. Praise the Lord!"

Mom concluded, "and He has called us as His own chosen children, even soldiers, in this spiritual warfare. And we are established in our faith. The only way you can stay established in your faith is to fill your heart with the Word of God. Amen! Not the commentary on the Word, but the Word! The living Word. The Word of God. Praise the Lord."

It was so encouraging and thrilling to know that we aren't in the Pentagon by chance, but we have been chosen and placed here for the very purpose of praying and interceeding for our nation and for our leaders. It was encouraging to think that the prayers of a small group of women could support great weight in the battle, the spiritual battle for our nation.

"God isn't finished with America yet," Ramona Jensen said. On staff with "Youth With A Mission" in Washington, D.C., for the America for Jesus rally, she visited our Ladies' Bible Class one noon hour. "Our present moral and spiritual condition is extremely bad and we must get serious with God. The unbelievers won't get serious, they've rejected Him. No, it's God's people who must get serious. They've got to stop playing church! They've got to stop living like the world around them, they've got to be willing to be 'different' and stand up for godliness and speak out against evil. God is raising up a people who will do just that!"

God sent another woman all the way from Anchorage, Alaska, to speak to our ladies group, and sure enough, Eva Evans told us the same message! "Don't think for one minute that you 'just happened' to take this job in the Pentagon, in the office where you work. God picked you out personally and put you in the midst of the worst kind of darkness." Eva laughed, "You don't buy a candle to put it in the sunshine, do you? No, you buy it to bring some light to a very dark place. You are the candle God has put in a dark office, to live righteously and honestly, in full view of people who ridicule and scoff at God's Word."

Another woman, on her first visit to our ladies' class, Caroline Shaefer told us "this tiny group of women is part of God's remnant. All through the Bible, God has His remnant. If any of you have ever done any sewing, you know that a remnant is just a tiny little bit. Well, God has all these people who have heard the Word, many who have even preached the Word and supposedly walked in the Word, but who will not yield themselves to His Holy Spirit and obey Him. Therefore, God clings to those few, those few even in Sardis. Those few even in Washington. Those few even in the Pentagon...who have heard the Word of God and have clung to the Word, and who long to be part of that tiny group, the remnant. Even in countries where you might be told "there are no Christians here," God can point to His little remnant."

I spoke up, in agreement with Caroline, "I was reading in Isaiah 14 and your message has made me think of how few there are, who really want to live for the Lord, to study His Word and become mature, not to remain babies. Here in this building there are people who will jog, shop, everything -- anything but going out for the Lord. You can tell of a prayer group and only a little handful will come. It's discouraging."

Caroline nodded, "You know at first this depresses you and you say, 'Oh, why don't more come?' But once you see that God knew all along this was how it was going to be...that there would be a small remnant that would be His people. But we have no right to feel superior to those people who don't long to hear the Word, because God put that hunger in our hearts. We should pray for that hunger and thirst for His Word. When you see someone that you really long to have hear the Word, and come to the Bible studies, and they just don't seem interested, pray for God to put that hunger in their hearts, because without it, they won't receive even if they come."

"You know we were depressed, too, because of some of the people we know who go to Bible studies and meetings every day, some of them all day sessions. We looked around and they were right back where they were when we met them! They hadn't grown. They hadn't gone any place in their walk with the Lord." Caroline continued, "We said, 'Lord, how can they hear all this and not do more than they are doing? And the Lord said to us, 'Feed my lambs.' You know all God cares about is what is in our hearts and whether we do what He says."

Caroline concluded, "Do believe in the remnant and strive to be part of it. The more you study the Word, the smaller the remnant gets! When I first heard this and began to read about it, I was shocked. But I have been increasingly shocked every day since. The remnant gets smaller and smaller. That is why I've said, sitting here in this room, is the remnant of God. Because in all the rest of this building, thousands of people are charging around, seeking the world and things of the world. This is why, in every place, wherever it is, no matter how much sin abides, in that place...God has His little group."

156

Such encouraging words! We just have to thank the Lord for the women that He has sent to our Pentagon Ladies' group, to encourage and remind us that we have a calling to pray for those in authority over us, that God places government in the hands of those He chooses. We knew from Daniel 4:32 that "the most high ruleth in the kingdom of men, and giveth it to whomsoever He will." We knew that much of what happens in America depends on whether we Christians will pray for godly and righteous leaders to rule over our land.

Were we "forgetful hearers" as the Bible mentions some people are? Is that why God has to send so many different women, at various times, to remind us of His call on our life?

"You are divinely placed, in order that you might be intercessors," Kay Colville told our ladies, as her opening remarks on her first of many visits. Kay is well known and much loved for her leadership of prayer groups in her home. In addition, Kay meets the needs of many Christians through her shops in the Washington area, known as "The Vine and the Fig Tree" bookstores.

"Give God no rest (Isaiah 62:7), as you seek His guidance, blessing and grace over this nation, and for those in authority over us. God has placed you here in this building and in this nation's capitol for this very purpose."

On another occasion, Caroline Shaefer told us that our ministry of prayer had brought our Pentagon group to her mind, as she read a book in which the author spoke of a prayer group amongst senior citizens. They were called Fanner Bees, reflecting the activities of this kind of Bee, whose duty was to fan the hive and keep the temperature regulated.

Caroline laughed, "The Fanner Bees are what keep it all going. In the book, they called those prayer warriors Fanner Bees, and if somebody had a need they'd quickly call the Fanner Bees and get them to go into prayer. When they'd all get into prayer, miraculous things would happen."

"I see you in this room as Fanner Bees, and when an office situation gets bad, call one of the Fanner Bees and put a "contract" on the ones who are causing the problem, that they will be able to speak nothing but love and turn the whole situation completely around!"

The ladies applauded and I laughed at the comparison, "we've got a new name for our group! Fanner Bees...I love it! We already do it, but we didn't have a name."

"They would be delighted to know the concept had passed along," Caroline said, "it's so wonderful to see the power, the power of prayer! But talk about Fanner Bees, we have got to seek the Lord. We've got to seek the Lord's blessings for our nation, that righteousness might be restored and seek His hand to guide and lead us once again. We've got to go to work!"

We thoroughly agreed with Caroline Shaefer, that we must be serious in our personal life and prayer life, to see our need for humbling ourselves and asking God's forgiveness and mercy on us individually and as a whole nation. Years ago, under Maidie's leadership, we selected a verse from the Bible as our motto. It was 2 Chronicles 7:14. "If my people, who are called by my name, will humble themselves and pray and seek my face and turn from their wicked ways, then I will hear from heaven and will forgive their sin and will heal their land."

Clearly God's Word said it would be His people who would humble themselves and pray and turn to Him. Then He would forgive their sin and heal their land. The ladies of the Pentagon Bible Classes took a day of their vacation leave to go as a group, and join with nearly one million Christians who gathered on the grassy mall near the nation's Capitol building. People had come at great expense and effort from Alaska, Hawaii, and every state in the union, to spend one day in fasting and prayer, seeking God's forgiveness and mercy on our great land. Many people ridiculed and some Christians refused to join in such a spectacle, feeling they should pray in their church and not on the streets. But God honored that act of repentance and turning to Him, and if there is a true and lasting change in attitudes and turning from sin to Him, the grace of God will be returned to America. We carried little signs that day, and it was our fervent prayer, "God bless America."

"God isn't finished with America yet -- He's just started," Bonnie Guiess told our ladies' group in September of 1980, when she was here visiting from the midwest. "The enemy wants to make us look bad, but he's a liar. He can't defeat us because there's more than ten righteous people here, right here in this room, and the fervent prayers of the righteous availeth much. Yes, they avail much. This building is protected because God's people are here praying! This building is full of angels, they are everywhere, ministering to you! If there is a report of a bomb in the building, begin to pray for the angels to come and help. Pray for them to find the bomb and take care of this building and these leaders. They'll do it! Whatever it is, fires or threats, the angels are sent to help you. Call on them. You don't see the angels, but you experience their protection."

Bonnie continued, "God has called you here, to the very front lines, to pray for our leaders, to pray for America. What you do here is very important. What goes on in this little Meditation Room is being recorded in God's books, and some day we will know what has been accomplished through prayer. You are "under cover agents" -- and the CIA doesn't know anything about you! You are in a position to protect the United States of America."

"You think you don't mean anything, but to God you mean everything! You think you're here because of your jobs. That is not so! You're here because God has put you here. God has a call on your life. That call is to begin to say what God has said, to speak forth His Word. And when you begin to speak 'Lord, I believe, I believe Your Word, I speak deliverance to your people, not only in America but to every situation affecting your people," when you begin to speak, God begins to move. God is moving across the land, deliverance and healing are in His hand! Don't let anybody tell you the bad reports, to you there is good news! When the bad news comes, measure it by the Word of God."

"You have no idea of the power of God that is resting in you," Bonnie assured the women gathered there for their lunch time, "you're an atomic bomb sitting here! By the Word of God you are. Not your ability that amounts to anything, it's His ability. You're His ambassador. He's put you here because He loves you. He has confidence in you. Maybe you don't have confidence in yourself, but He does! He knows you because you belong to Him. In this building, may grace and truth walk through every room and every hall and into every closet."

"Pray about everything that has to do with America, that has to do with the world, that has to do with what God wants for His people." Bonnie concluded, "Go to the Father, pray for our leaders to walk in holiness. Ask God to give our leaders great wisdom, that they'll be meek and humble and their hearts would be set for God's love and the good of His people, that we will walk in peace. Pray that all things that the enemy has taken away, God would restore to America. Above all, place over it the name of Jesus, the name above every name."

Here it was again...the same message! We knew it had to be God! There was no way these women could know what the other person had said to us. No way they could have agreed on what to tell us, yet each one had told us that we weren't in the Pentagon by chance, that we'd been chosen and placed here.

Why? I'm not sure, of course. Perhaps because we've found prayer isn't idle words, nor a ritual. Perhaps because we've found that there is power when several agree and pray together. Perhaps because we have decided we'd rather pray than eat! Whatever the reason, we're glad to be chosen. What a privilege to be able to pray for America, to be chosen to pray.

"America, America, God shed His grace on thee." That is our prayer and our heart's cry to God. When I think of how a land can be when God sheds His grace on it, I am reminded of a "truly happy land" described in Psalms 144:12-15 in the Living Bible. It is a happy and blessed land because God is revered and acknowledged over all. The results of God's blessing are:

The barns are full, plenty of livestock and produce!

No enemy is attacking from outside the land, and peace is everywhere!

No crime is in the streets! Nor complaining!

The young men are vigorous and mature.

The women are beautiful and supportive, like pillars of a palace.

Yes, truly happy are those whose God is the Lord.

This scripture made me think of God's women, who were described as pillars. But who ever notices a pillar? Rarely do you glance at one, it is almost unnoticed. Yet vital. And that describes our praying women, God's women. Unnoticed, yet supporting America, like pillars...the **Pillars of the Pentagon.**

159